CW00747534

Called into Exile…

… between the Stones and the Firelight:

Book 2

Mark Tanner

LITTLE HOUSE IN
- JOPPA -

Little House in Joppa Publishing
Abbey Street, Chester, CH1 2JD, UK
admin@little-house-in-joppa.uk

Copyright © Mark Tanner 2023

All rights reserved. No part of this publication may be reproduced,
distributed, or transmitted in any form or by any means, including
photocopying, recording, or other electronic or mechanical methods,
without the prior written permission of the publisher, except in the
case of brief quotations embodied in critical reviews and certain
other non-commercial uses permitted by copyright law. For
permission requests, write to the publisher, addressed 'Copyright
administrator, Little House at Joppa' at the address above.

Every effort has been made to trace copyright holders and obtain
permission for the use of any copyrighted material. The publisher
apologises for any errors or omissions and would be grateful to be
notified of any corrections that should be incorporated in future
reprints of this book.

Scripture quotations, unless otherwise specified are from New
Revised Standard Version Bible: Anglicized Edition,
copyright © 1989, 1995 National Council of the Churches of Christ in
the United States of America. Used by permission.
All rights reserved worldwide.

First edition: 2023
ISBN: 978-1-7392688-1-7

DEDICATION

For those who have given me the confidence to read, to think, to pray, and to be honest about what I encounter...

... for those who, in so doing, have led me back to Jesus' feet and enabled me to keep returning...

... I cannot ever thank you enough.

INDEX

PREFACE TO THE FIRST EDITION

This is the second book in a series of three, and I confess that it is the one that energises me most. I love the things we consider in the other two, but this one sets my imagination racing every time I come back to it. The simple insight at the heart of the book unlocks vast and varied riches for practical living as Christ-followers in the 'stuff' of daily normality.

As I explained in Book 1, *Clinging to the Cross*[1], this is material which began as my own reflections as I thought and prayed through my increasing uneasiness at the impasse we appeared to be reaching about questions of sexuality in the church. It soon became more than this as I (re)encountered Jesus side-stepping the dilemmas that seem to threaten to sink our own theologising. We face a storm; he sleeps, and when he wakes (if we dare wake him), he merely commands the storm to be still. We come up against red lines; he redraws them in blood and speaks grace. We bump into hard boundaries and seek differentiation; he breaks down dividing walls. We struggle with conflict; he is our peace.

How do we 'do' faithfulness in complexity? How do we do kindness and clarity in a Christlike way?

---

[1] Available through little-house-in-joppa.uk/home

Meeting Jesus changes everything for all who meet him. Here we search the scriptures to explore what we can learn about exilic faithfulness which follows Christ into the wider world and does not get lost, drowned, or broken.

I offer this series in the midst of the Church of England's *Living in Love and Faith* (LLF) project. I publish it in this form for the Diocese for which I care here in Chester, UK. It engages with many issues, but the ground covered by LLF is part of what it considers. Publishing timings don't normally allow for this speed of delivery, but I can offer this slightly more rough and ready, less edited version, and thus do so with humility.

The material is, of course, available to anyone. It is not constrained to this diocese, although that is the reason it comes out now and in this form. You are welcome whoever you are as you read, and I pray you will meet with Christ as you do.

Please forgive typos (you are welcome to point them out if you wish, sending them to corrections@little-house-in-joppa.uk with book title, format, and page number), and please remember that this is thinking which is still in process for me as well as for you.

I have kept the pattern of offering questions for reflection at the end of each of the main chapters. This is, partly, because groups might like to use this material as study material. It also, though, helps readers engage with this material devotionally.

I pray that, as you read, reflect, and wrestle with the complexity of faithfulness in exile, you will not only find your own faith deepened, you will be released into deeper fellowship and ever more graceful freedom.

God bless you, once again, as you inhabit this place which we are coming to know as the space between the Stones and the Firelight.

† Mark
March 2023

PROLOGUE

You might like to listen to this before reading on
(it was designed to be heard more than read), but it's up to
you.

Today is the day. I remember thinking that... all those years ago... it feels like a different life now. I don't know what kind of a day I thought it was going to be, but today was going to be the day.

Not in my dreams, or even in my terrors, my living nightmares. I don't know if you'll get this, but the terrors were so much more frightening when I had no home, and no family, and no-one who cared at all about anything more than how much I could nick for them or how little I had nicked from them.

But today... on that today... something needed to happen. I guess the religious people would have pretended that it all just happened as it needed to, in that singsong pretty-voice way they have when they make dreadful things sound right and as if God himself required them. Belongers who seem terrified that they might not belong enough, and push others away in their own scramble to belong. Preachers of peace just stirring up trouble.

It was just that kind of day: it was going to explode. The tension had been bubbling and building, and now it was going to boil over. You just pick these things up when you live on the streets. It's a kind of sense you develop without trying.

The city speaks, and if you are wise you listen. And today, we needed some relief from all the tension. Someone to hate and mock and climb all over as we all tried to reassure ourselves that we are better than them at least. Someone further away from home than I am so I don't feel so bad about my loneliness. I remember thinking how odd that the posh gits seem to feel it too. Although do they? They are not half as clever as they seem to think, you know.

I had kind of gone to ground in the way that we do. Straighten your hair. Fold my smock to hide the worst of the stains. Only take what I need to get by today. I was lucky that I was still only a boy, and a small one at that, with wide eyes and a cheeky grin.

To be honest, when I saw it, I was just glad it was not me who'd been nabbed at first.

And then I saw what the fuss was about, and...

... well to be honest I am ashamed of myself looking back.

I was thrilled! A screaming woman with virtually nothing on being dragged through the streets by those pompous priesty pillocks in all their finery. You should have heard her language! And no-one expected her to be able to hit a religious bloke that hard. Idiot! He should have been able to duck that one. Her terrors were real; although I was not going to think of that - I had enough of my own.

Strangely, though, they were clearly looking for him. As if one fight were not enough in a day. No, that's not how it felt... as if this fight were really an excuse for that fight.

They gathered.

They shouted.

She cowered.

We gawked.

It was amazing...

... and it was horrible.

And we all knew what to expect.

The soldiers would turn up in a moment just like they always did when things got fruity. Oh, there might be a couple of stones thrown, but what did they care if there was the odd broken bone or black eye? If we were lucky there might be a full blown riot and then the pickings would be really great. I could rest for a month after that kind of day.

It was perfect.

A perfect moment of opportunity for chaos as we found we were gathered around that quiet, seated figure... so still in the restless hubbub.

So still as he wrote on the floor in that odd and calm way.

So still, you could not help but to notice.

So oddly still as he spoke.

And the perfect puzzle scrawled on their faces was priceless...

And the perfect awfulness of seeing what we were about to do now seems just soul-destroyingly achingly broken...

And the perfect look on that face, her face, her face which had looked as I so often feel, her face which now looked up... as she looked at him for the very first time. I want that look. The look of dream replacing terror, but somehow more certain than that has ever been.

And off she was sent...

... to leave that life...

... and off I went as all went quiet...

... on the outside at least...

... and I stumbled into a whole new day, beginning to realise that for me, those streets would never be the same again.

Could it be that this is all that is needed? That this is where belonging belongs? That this little homeless little runt might have spotted a different way of surviving? If it was true for her...

That there might be something to grow into. Something for that smile to actually embrace. That I might one day come home?

The city is not sure what to make of this, but today I dream a different dream. A dream unconstrained by the shadows of terror which does not yet know how to stretch its wings and might not need to steal in order to survive. A dream of actual, proper grace. A real, can it be a real, dream? A dream realised in the eyes of the one who left to leave her old life... and held in the eyes of the one who freed her.

Today is that day..

Note about the reflections...

... which follow the pattern set in *Clinging to the Cross* (Book 1 of this Stones and the Firelight series), and are more fully explained there. Here, too, we will start with a perspective on the woman about to be stoned and end up reflecting on Peter's journey between two fireplaces. These reflections border the space that we explore in the three great biblical themes held in these books; they set the tone, shape the exploring, and root us in the biblical text. They are designed to be heard, rather than read (and hence the QR codes which take you to a recorded version of each one).

Please allow these reflections to invite you into the presence of Christ. I have written each as a stand-alone piece, but positioned them to open up our thinking/praying/reflecting on each section and to enable us to be shaped by the scriptures. Do listen and try to listen with your head, your heart, and your soul, but also pause and dwell for a moment in the text. This is an ancient way of reading the Bible with some of the work done for you. St Ignatius of Loyola set out ways of doing 'Lectio Divina' (Godly reading) which help us inhabit the biblical text (although the practice of Lectio is based on the ways Jews read the scriptures at Passover and has been part of Christian practice since St Gregory of Nyssa taught about it in the 4th Century). These reflections are simply some of my written lectios offered to you. Your own readings will be just as valid, possibly even more so. May mine, though, be a springboard into each section of this book, an invitation and a spur into further engagement.

INTRODUCTION

_____

As you pick up this book you join us part way through a journey. Each stage of that journey has its own logic and rhythm and can be taken as an adventure in its own right, but it does sit within a bigger whole. For some, this will appear to be a series of reflections around human sexuality, but it is intended to be much more and much less than that. It is not offered as 'an answer', but rather as a way of prayer, reflection, and finding hope in Christ. It sets out to explore territory which we can inhabit together with each other and with him as we wrestle with difficult issues.

I describe this space as being 'between the stones and the firelight', because in complexity we are called to inhabit a bounded space, where the boundaries matter but are not grace-filled places to dwell. The edges contain the space and sometimes feel certain, but the space itself is spacious, less tightly held, and utterly real . The woman caught in adultery from John 8 (where was the man who must, presumably, have been party to this activity? I always wonder) presents us with the kind of judgemental response we often find within ourselves. Here we should be shocked at Jesus' extraordinary kindness and ability to liberate, but always need to remember that this is the start of a journey which continues with every step she takes away from the place of that encounter. Peter, seen in the light of the fire in the courtyard and the fire on the beach, is a picture of frail dependence on Christ. How can it be that the church should be built on the insecure foundations that Peter seems to offer?

In the previous book we looked at the cross and how this informs our living faithfully, our search for holiness, and our missional relating. These three areas, faithfulness, holiness, and mission spur me on in writing as I try to live well as a Christian in complex times. In one way, I don't think that it matters very much what the complex issue is that we are wrestling with in this regard, the question is where we go to resource ourselves for that faithful living.

In this book we continue the same journey, coming back to the theme of exile which is absolutely core to the biblical narrative but often overlooked in Christian teaching. If the cross invites us into this in-between, holding-on space, exile teaches us how we live here, and our explorations of powerlessness in Book 3 will begin to help us consider what type of people we need to be in this space. The three central questions remain though:

How do I remain faithful?

For me, everything starts here. How do I remain faithful to Christ? It is so easy to approach the question of faithfulness by beginning with loyalty to my brothers and sisters in faith (and that deeply matters), but the fundamental starting point must be Jesus. The most precious gift of writing this material for me, as I have already described, has been the space and the encouragement to come back to the Bible and allow myself the freedom to live with questions without needing to respond immediately to the many urgent voices consciously or subconsciously pressing their answers onto me.

I have reflected a little on my suspicion that the Holy Spirit is doing more among us, in this day, than drawing us to think about sexuality. One of my daily experiences (pretty much literally at the moment) is receiving impassioned letters and e-mails in which the author sets out a case with regard to sexuality; most seem sensible, gracious, and utterly convinced. The letters are marked by a number of similarities, though:

they tend to appear to assume I have not thought about the issues well enough, that I do not really understand the Bible or Christian tradition, that I have little compassion for others, that most people agree with them, and that the author knows my own views on the matters in hand. They differ in that they express radically different views to other letters I receive on the same day. Equal conviction, equal reference to scripture, equal desire to share faith with others, equal desire for me to agree with their view, and radically different views.

These are not easy to read, and I sometimes joke that there is a remarkable freedom that comes from knowing you will be despised whatever you decide when you have to make a decision. In this place it is vital that we take time to ask what really matters, and what matters here is faithfulness to Christ.

How do we stand together?

However, I am not comfortable leaving that last thought where I have. This can be how it feels, but we cannot write each other off and we cannot ignore the insights that others give. The truth is that we cannot live the Christian life alone, and we cannot find wisdom without the gift of others.

Unity matters on so many levels and we shall return to this at the end of the third book in this series at far greater length. One of the many things that we see, though, as we consider the theme of exile is that we do not need to agree about everything in order to stand together…

… and unless we stand together we will find that we cannot begin to be the people we are called to be.

How do we share this good news?

Finally, we must be true to the priorities of the one who calls and commands us, and we have explored (at the end of Book 1) the importance of mission in this regard.

In truth, I don't think I could exaggerate or overemphasise the way in which our feuding as Christians pushes people away from Jesus. When we claim to have good news and live apparently bad news, preach peace and seem to inhabit conflict, proclaim love and harbour what feels like hatred, or postulate about grace in a manner which is received as anything but gracious, we cannot be surprised when people look elsewhere for hope. People simply are not interested in a theoretical gospel, but they are deeply hungry to be loved.

As you explore with this book, please allow yourself to be drawn into this set of questions, for they matter very profoundly.

Our basic metaphor

Our basic metaphor in this book is exile. Please note that I describe it as a metaphor: it is a learning tool, a picture, a representation of reality. I am not suggesting that Christians do not belong (in fact quite the reverse). This is not simplistic and there are some complexities we will explore, but it is relatively straightforward.

Before we get fully into it there are some introductory things that I want to note. One is more general and concerns the way that we talk about difficult issues, because our language is very rarely neutral. It is often (perhaps always, but I am not sure that I can assert that with certainty) going to be part of the problem or part of the solution when we face a challenge. We come back to our words in a moment.

First, though, let me note two quick things: an insight and a corrective about exile.

A basic insight about the Bible

I think I first stumbled over this when delivering Alpha courses: things which are true physically under the first covenant are often true spiritually in the second. In other words, things that we see enacted in bodily form in the Old Testament are commonly matters of the heart, soul, or life in the New Testament. This would be true, for example, of circumcision. On the eighth day Jewish boys are circumcised[2]. This is not a metaphor; it involved a real blade, a real foreskin, and a lasting change to the body. It is true that the metaphorical implications were clear with instruction to 'circumcise your hearts[3]' being given in the Torah, but circumcision is not simply an idea. In Acts 15 the requirement for Christians to be (physically) circumcised is rejected, and in writing to the church in Galatia Paul goes even further in teaching that they must not be circumcised[4]. However, there is a circumcision which is an essential part of being Christian, and is 'performed by Christ' when you come to him[5]. It is not physical, but it is real and it is spiritual and it marks us as eternal members of the new covenant people of God.

The same would be true of the promised land: it is a real earthy this-world land for the people of Israel, whereas it is a coming promise for the people of Christ. It is true of food requirements, which are literal for the Jew and concern what you eat, whereas the Christian is concerned for what goes in and out of the person[6] in an altogether more holistic way.

It is in this sense that we will be discussing exile. I am not talking about being physical refugees, living far from our place of birth, or under foreign rule (at least in the sense of our human and worldly existence). I am talking about the eternal, soulish, spiritual reality of our lives. We will seek to learn from the physical theme of exile as seen in the first covenant described in the Old Testament, but need to make the leap into our bigger reality in Christ.

---

[2] See Genesis 17, for example
[3] See Deuteronomy 10.16 or Deuteronomy 30.6, for example
[4] Galatians 5.2
[5] Colossians 2.11
[6] See Matthew 15.17-18

And a corrective

It might be easy to misunderstand me quite fundamentally if you hear me describe our current exile as some kind of exile from the 'church' or 'the Kingdom' because we have to live in the wider world. Let me be very clear that God is at work in our world today: this is his theatre of operations and he has not abandoned it. We are not necessarily sullied by engaging in the wider world as Christians, or being punished because we must live here. However, this is also not what we were ultimately created for. The Lord will return. We will live as we have been created to live in all fulness of life. This, though, is not (fully) here yet. It is this patient distanced waiting that I am referring to as exile.

It is a challenge, but it is also an invitation.

A word about words

> Sticks and stones may break my bones
> But words can tear my heart out [7]

The other thing that I want to reflect upon before we dive into this material is something about the way we talk about the stuff with which we wrestle and the way we talk about each other in our wrestling. Words are both far more powerful than we realise and far less significant than we think. When it comes to living well with difference between sisters and brothers in Christ it is vital that we recognise and reflect on this, at least a little.

This is not a complicated thought, although I keep accidentally making it so. I am not a theorist when it comes to communication, and I don't want to make an academic or rhetorical case. I just want to point out the obvious and prompt you to reflect to help us live better when it comes to living in complexity. Some relatively simple observations in this regard

---

[7] *Poem remembered from a Steve Turner performance at Greenbelt in the 1980s*

might help us live well in the territory explored in this book. You are a daily practitioner of the art of communication, just as I am: I hope that what I say makes sense to you and that you can make use of it.

Words communicate

At a very basic level, words are there to communicate. I have just been on holiday to Wales, and for interest and out of respect I have been learning a bit of Welsh. It is both fun and satisfying to go into a coffee shop and ask for a cuppa and an ice-cream to be brought to table 14 in Welsh and be understood. That is what words do even when you are not fluent and you have to ask for a translation of the reply.

Right now (in my world), I am typing words. Right now (in your world), you are reading them. The timeframes of those two worlds are different, they might be a few months apart or you could be reading these words hundreds or thousands of years after they were written. The words communicate. However, what if you are reading them with them having been translated into Welsh? Is it my actual words that communicate, or the translators', or maybe the thinking behind them which the words seek to grasp and hand on? In truth it is often all of this and more; words capture something that is beyond them, a thought, feeling, or experience, for example, and express it. Well-crafted words might do so profoundly evocatively, and less eloquent words might simply get the basic idea across, but all words communicate something.

Christians hold the Bible to be the Word of God. It is written, and translated, in order that we might hear God's voice. We hold words to be of vital importance to our faith, and we know that we must work to understand them.

Words express who we are

More than this, though, words give expression to the person behind the words. In reading this you will be getting to know me a little. Listen to two people talking about exactly the same thing and you will hear two different voices (literally, but also metaphorically); you will meet two different people.

There are all sorts of reasons for this, and they go beyond the scope of this brief chapter. It is partly what people talk about, partly the way they talk about it, partly the terms and expressions that they choose to use. As we note below, it is partly the non-verbal cues that they give (what they look like, their expression, tone of voice, and many other things besides) which communicate, but the point is that we meet the person as we hear the words.

Again, this matters for Christians, as we believe that Jesus *is* the Word of God as well as the primary One who speaks the words of God. He is the image of the invisible God[8]. He is the visible expression of who God is: meet him and you are meeting God himself.

Words shape us

Perhaps not surprisingly, words shape who we are. Some 'words' hang around us. Encourage a child as they act kindly, and you often nurture a caring spirit for life. Tell a child that they are fat or ugly often enough and you run a profound risk of them living with that conviction for the rest of their days. The child who is less good at football in the playground might be spurred into extensive practice by their classmates' mockery... or they might be cemented for life into an inability to control a ball at their feet (not that I am bitter at all).

Words shape us when they are spoken to us, but they also shape us in the speaking. I have explored in another book some of the reasons that the Bible commands us not to complain and how it changes us when we take this seriously[9]. We have seen in wider society over the last few decades how oppressive language fosters oppressive attitudes and practice: sexist jokes encourage everyday sexism, quiet racist comments between

---

[8] Colossians 1.15
[9] See my other work on vocation.

friends reinforce endemic racism, mockery of disability spreads the myth that particular physical or mental difference somehow devalues the humanity of the disabled person. Compare the comedy shown on the BBC in the 1970s with today's broadcast humour, contrast Benny Hill with Michael McIntyre for example, and it is clear just how far we have come in this regard.

Again, this is not a surprise to Christians. There is an ancient saying used in churches like the Church of England, 'lex orandi, lex credendi', meaning 'as we pray, so we believe'. This is why liturgy matters so much (it matters in all churches, it is just that some write it down, others allow musicians to set it to music, and others simply settle into patterns of speech and action). We repeat truths about our faith and they shape what we believe[10].

Words, then, are really important. We need to attend to what we say and the way that we say it. However, and at the same time, words are far more limited and sometimes less helpful than we might like to think.

Words communicate only a part of what we want to say

We are more sensitive to this than we might usually realise. Few of us will fail to recall times when we are sure that we are being lied to. Someone's words say one thing, but their actions,

---

[10] Incidentally, this is why we ought to be far more careful about the lyrics of the worship songs that we sing. Songs are sometimes chosen for the music, not for their theology or even logic, and hilarious idiocy can be ignored, repeated, and imbibed. Sometimes this is simply irritating or funny, for example, suggesting that a lighthouse can carry us or that it guides to safety when the whole point of a real lighthouse is exactly the opposite. Sometimes this is plain dangerous: suggesting that God is 'fighting *our* battles' as Mooring, Johnson and Gifford Brown do in the otherwise amazing song 'The Lion and the Lamb' has some bigger theological truth but seems worryingly misleading in a self-oriented consumer world like ours.

their body language, their tone of voice all communicate something else and we end up not believing the words. I often think about this when I greet my dog (not that I am comparing anyone to my dog, you understand, even though she is amazing): it is childish but amusing to wander into the kitchen when we get home and make a fuss of her, ruffling her fur, stroking her, speaking in warm and excited tones that match her joy at seeing us, and telling her that she is a stinky horrible beast and that she knows how much we hate her (we really don't hate her and whilst she does reek occasionally she is lovely). She wags her tail and 'hears' the tone, the action, the affection, and the playfulness. The words mean nothing to her at all, the communication means everything.

The same basic principle is true for humans, even though it is infinitely more nuanced. That is why you cannot talk your way out of a situation you have behaved your way into. It is why words can be 'empty'. It is why relationship matters if we are to communicate. It is why listening matters at least as much, probably more, than speaking when it comes to words. And by listening, of course, I mean so much more than hearing: I mean attending, considering, pondering, and seeking to understand. I mean noticing the poetry, allowing another to do their best at expressing something which is beyond the limits of a sound, and meeting them on the journey of understanding what is being expressed. Words are the stepping stones that enable infinity to be crossed and souls to meet, and they are beautiful for it, but they are not the real beauty or wonder: that resides in the depths of the other and is in the image of God.

Words, in our manipulative, spin-obsessed, post truth society are easily employed and we are wise to be alert to integrity in those speaking to us. We know how to do this from being tiny babies: long before we understand the words spoken to us we understand some deep truths about what people are saying.

Words are not the end goal of communication

The end goal of our speech or our writing is (almost always) communication; our words are merely one tool deployed in order to enable one person to express something that exists internally to one or more others. They can be stunningly beautiful, deeply profound, and exquisitely crafted at times, even to the extent of being appreciated as art in and of themselves, but their basic function remains that of facilitating communication.

The reason I point out this obvious truth (using words to do it, ironically) is that those of us who seek to communicate take on some degree of responsibility for how we are heard as well as what we say. Those who cross cultural barriers face this all the time: one hand signal might express appreciation in one culture and profound insult in another. Raising your voice in one place may express passion, but be deeply offensive in another. If you are in a country foreign to you and someone is kind enough to speak to you in your own language, limited though their grasp of it may be, you will employ simpler words and speak slower than when speaking to a professional in a field you know well. If you want people to understand you adapt the way you communicate.

Teachers practise this as they shape their lessons to improve the practice and comprehension of the class in front of them. Preachers reflect on it all the time (or at least, they should reflect on it). It does not ultimately matter what a preacher says, what matters is what they are heard to say, how people understood it, and how those hearers are enabled to respond to God as a result.

Words of disagreement

This matters when it comes to living well in disagreement. We can feel we need to defend ourselves, and that can be helpful to an extent. We do need to work on ways of clearly expressing our perspective if we are to contribute to the debates we are having, but we also need to be alert to what our words say about who we are and the impact they have on others. We will talk at the beginning of Book 3[11] about the place of emotion in difficult conversations, but here I want to make the point that disagreement will sometimes limit what can be said at a particular time or in a particular conversation.

Sometimes I will be so hurt by an issue that all I can hear from those who disagree with me is that I am hated. I may or may not be hated, but unless and until I can understand that I am not, I am unlikely to be able to hear anything else others say that disagrees with me.

This will mean that your ability to communicate will depend not on your ability to express yourself but on the depth of loving commitment you have to me. I may not have the ability to hear (or sometimes even be able to bear the cost, or take the pain of hearing) the things that you feel you have the right to say. Say them and leave if you will, but please don't feel you have communicated to me.

There is an old adage that says that what most people need is a jolly good listening to.

There are times, as we stand together in complexity and disagreement, that listening is all we can do if we are committed to loving each other, and only then will we begin stumblingly and hesitantly to find the right words to explore the territory we need to cover together. The words that we find in this place really matter. I think it was Winnie the Pooh who observed that sometimes the smallest things take up the most room in our heart. Gentle, risky, and humble words offered kindly can feel tiny but they change the world.

In that place of kind communication we will finally be free to be real, to be undefended, to be gentle, to be loving and loved, known, trusted, and at home. In this place, even in small ways

---

[11] See little-house-in-joppa.uk/home for details of this book as it becomes available

that feel like they have little to do with faith we begin to encounter the risk of the incarnation afresh. Words are very powerful and the way we say what we need to say matters.

This matters in every situation, but perhaps particularly when we find (or feel) ourselves to be strangers in a strange place and look to each other for fellowship. This is the common experience of the exile through the ages and the Bible has extensive wisdom for us in these times.

BOOK TWO: CALLED INTO EXILE

1 - REFLECTION

You might like to listen to this before reading on
(it was designed to be heard more than read), but it's up to you.

I know that I should have done more... I just really don't know how.

All I can hear running around my head is the voice of old Master Shemuel as he taught the Bible to us: beware the lure of other gods, boys: it's a slippery slope to idolatry, blasphemy. You just remember who you are and how strictly God judges the faithless.

I was 12 years old, for goodness sake! Those Babylonian hordes: they were overwhelming, terrifying. What strange and Godless people they seemed. These Babylonian hordes: they are a mighty impressive people you know. Their art. Their poetry. Their culture. Their learning. And, I hate to admit it, but I have thrived here. I think this might be who I am: fluent, smart, leadership material apparently.

And a Jew.

A little Jewish boy by the name of 'May the god Bel protect his life', Belteshazzar, a little covenant child of the one true and living God, marked for life on the eighth day of life: dressed, named, behaving for all the world like a ruling child of the Babylonian elite. And I love it here!

Can I even say that?

Remember who you are. That was the instruction at school when I was a boy.

It was so odd at first here. The language. The way they dressed. And their temples... did they not know how wrong it was? It is, I should say.

I don't think it's so odd now, of course. I have learned so much over the years. My folks would be proud of me... well at least I think my folks would be proud of me... well at least I like to think they would be if only they understood... which they probably wouldn't really now I think of it. My world is so different to anything they knew. I quite like it now, if I am really honest. Even the temple stuff: I know it is wrong, but, boy, it is beautiful. The music is sublime. And the eloquence of the priests... it makes the spine tingle if you listen to it. The way they weave the poets alongside the insights of the philosophers. I got top grades on my philosophy paper, don't you know, even winning the King's Award! Sometimes it feels like I am so at home here. That they are right and this really is who I am.

But I am a Jew. That is my identity. Not this.

And so came the food.

Everyone is blown away by my choice to become teetotal and a vegetarian: like it is heroic or something. But that's not me. I even asked permission before trying it and if God had not blessed our plan we would have been forced back to the steaks and red wine. Tough gig, eh?

Who am I?

I am a Jew.

I am in exile.

I am in Babylon and I am very very good at it.

I am a Jew, and one day I might do better at it.

I am Daniel. I am Belteshazzar. I am me.

I should have done so much more... I just really don't know how.

2 - EXILE: THE LIFE OF FAITH

Often the solitary one finds grace for himself
[in] the mercy of the Lord[12]

The question we need to explore is how we live in this place of in-between-ness; this place of holding on to the world and to the Lord, of speaking a message of hope in a language which can be heard. What models do we have from scripture, reason, and tradition which will enable us to live and love a world which is broken and divergent from God's way?

One approach, which is the one that we explore in this book, is to consider how the people of God have been called to live when in exile. We see this theme prominently throughout the Hebrew Scriptures, where the people of God are often found far from the promised land and outside the Kingdom. It has long seemed to me that it is a great strand of Biblical Theology which is largely missing from our Christian work in popular ethics, at least in the modern Western world. This is troubling both because it misses vast amounts of wisdom that we could imbibe, but also because it flirts with the idea that authentic Christian life is somehow to inhabit a kind of new 'promised land' within which the will of God is perfectly enacted. (In the first book I argued that this is not consonant with the Scriptural injunctions although I recognise that the concept is tempting: we shall return to this later.)

There are some fascinating early English poems indicating that exile was once a biblical concept which was much more embraced, but it does seem to be an area of insight we now

---

[12] 'The Wanderer', in translation – see little-house-in-joppa.uk/ S&F202334

largely overlook. Listen for a moment to some of the late 10th century Anglo-Saxon poem, The Wanderer, from which I quote above. Printed words cannot fully capture the longing and angst, of course, but, they are haunting and powerful even after all these centuries. The poem begins:

Oft him anhaga	*Often the solitary one*
are gebideð,	*waits for grace*
metudes miltse,	*the mercy of the Lord,*
þeah þe he modcearig	*Although he, sorry-hearted,*
geond lagulade	*must for a long time*
longe sceolde	*move by hand*
	[in context = row]
hreran mid hondum	*along the waterways,*
hrimcealde sæ	*(along) the ice-cold sea,*
wadan wræclastas.	*tread the paths of exile.*
Wyrd bið ful aræd!	*Events always go*
	as they must!
Swa cwæð eardstapa,	*So spoke the wanderer,*
earfeþa gemyndig,	*mindful of hardships,*
wraþra wælsleahta,	*of fierce slaughters*
winemæga hryre:	*and the downfall of kinsmen:*
Oft ic sceolde ana	*Often (or always) I had alone*
uhtna gehwylce	*to speak of my trouble*
mine ceare cwiþan.	*each morning before dawn.*
Nis nu cwicra nan	*There is none now living*
þe ic him modsefan	*to whom I dare*
minne durre	*clearly speak*
sweotule asecgan.	*of my innermost thoughts.*
Ic to soþe wat	*I know it truly,*
þæt biþ in eorle	*that it is in men*
indryhten þeaw,	*a noble custom,*
þæt he his ferðlocan	*that one should keep secure*
fæste binde,	*his spirit-chest (mind),*
healde his hordcofan,	*guard his treasure-chamber*
	(thoughts),
hycge swa he wille.	*think as he wishes.*
Ne mæg werig mod	*The weary spirit cannot*

wyrde wiðstondan,	withstand fate (the turn of events),
ne se hreo hyge	nor does a rough or sorrowful mind
helpe gefremman.	do any good (perform anything helpful).
Forðon domgeorne	Thus those eager for glory
dreorigne oft	often keep secure
in hyra breostcofan	dreary thoughts
bindað fæste;	in their breast;
swa ic modsefan	So I,
minne sceolde,	often wretched and sorrowful,
oft earmcearig,	bereft of my homeland,
eðle bidæled,	far from noble kinsmen,
freomægum feor	have had to bind in fetters
feterum sælan,	my inmost thoughts,

The unknown poet continues:

Eall is earfoðlic	All is troublesome
eorþan rice,	in this earthly kingdom,
onwendeð wyrda gesceaft	the turn of events changes
weoruld under heofonum.	the world under the heavens.
Her bið feoh læne,	Here money is fleeting,
her bið freond læne,	here friend is fleeting,
her bið mon læne,	here man is fleeting,
her bið mæg læne,	here kinsman is fleeting,
eal þis eorþan gesteal	all the foundation of this world
idel weorþeð!	turns to waste!

Swa cwæð snottor on mode,	So spake the wise man in his mind,
gesæt him sundor æt rune.	where he sat apart in counsel.
Til biþ se þe his treowe gehealdeþ,	Good is he who keeps his faith,
ne sceal næfre his torn to rycene	And a warrior must never speak
beorn of his breostum acyþan,	his grief of his breast too quickly,
nemþe he ær þa bote cunne,	unless he already knows the remedy -
eorl mid elne gefremman.	a hero must act with courage.

Wel bið þam þe him are seceð,	*It is better for the one that seeks mercy,*
frofre to Fæder on heofonum,	*consolation from the father in the heavens,*
þær us eal seo fæstnung stondeð.	*where, for us, all permanence rests.*[13]

So spoke the wanderer... *it is better for the who that seeks mercy [and] consolation from the Father in the heavens, where, for us all permanence rests.* There is a great deal we need to reclaim and re-ponder in this theme of exile, but we are not the first to tread these paths and we would be wise to learn from others who have walked them before us. I note, in passing for now, my own appreciation of the fact that it is in poetry that we glimpse our English heritage in reflecting on this area. There are rational facts we must consider, and practical ways we may respond, but if we do not engage in the emotionally intelligent work of our vocation to exile we will not live well or fruitfully in these times. I am very far from expert (by which I mean that I am a complete beginner) when it comes to Early English poetry, but I find the encapsulation of faith, feeling, and reflection in these words captivating, rich, and apposite.

Exile: a biblical overview

Think of the broad overview of the scriptural narrative: in the first covenant (the one with Israel set out in the Hebrew Scriptures within which the Jewish people live both historically and spiritually) the basic story is that the people of God are given the promised land of the covenant and there they remain while they are faithful. The pattern is axiomatic, clear, and prescribed: when they stray or rebel they are warned by the prophets and called back to obedience to the covenant.

---

[13] Ibid (except line 2 of modern English translation, which is courtesy of Amy Dorward of Exeter College, Oxford, to whom I express my gratitude for this and for alerting me to these poems)

Ultimately, though, God will allow them to be taken into exile in what he intends as a kind of ultimate wake-up call. Exile is a place intended for repentance and restoration.

> Just like the clay in the potter's hand, so are you in my hand, O house of Israel. At one moment I may declare concerning a nation or a kingdom, that I will pluck up and break down and destroy it, but if that nation, concerning which I have spoken, turns from its evil, I will change my mind about the disaster that I intended to bring on it.[14]

In the new covenant of the Christ (under which we live as Christians and which is set out in the New Testament) it might appear that exile is no longer part of the life of faith... at least at first sight. Christians are not usually literal exiles in the nations where they are citizens, at least in the West. (I am a British citizen, living in the UK, and being a Christian does not take away any of my rights or responsibilities.) Nor is there some kind of here-and-now promised land for Christians. The world we inhabit is the world in which God is currently at work. We are not 'saved out of the world', although we are saved for a new world.

First sight, though, is not enough. The basic narrative of the New Testament is that God, in Christ...

> ... did not regard equality with God as something to be exploited, but emptied himself, taking the form of a slave, being born in human likeness. And being found in human form, he humbled himself and became obedient to the point of death— even death on a cross.[15]

God chooses, in the incarnation, to inhabit a space other than the immediate presence of the Father in order that we might find salvation. Moreover, when he comes he teaches about the coming Kingdom of God in a manner that makes it very clear that it is our inheritance in him but that it is not here, yet, in all its fulness. And what is the reason that this place, to which we

---

[14] Jeremiah 18.6b-8
[15] Philippians 2.6-8

now belong and where there will be *'no more weeping or gnashing of teeth[16]'*, where the *'wolf will live with the lamb, the leopard lie down with the kid... and a little child shall lead them[17]'*? The reason is not that God is slow or stingy, such that we need to earn our way into the promised land. It is so that as many as possible might find forgiveness and come, like the errant prodigal of Luke 15, back to the Father's embrace and all that he has for them.

> *The Lord is not slow about his promise, as some think of slowness, but is patient with you, not wanting any to perish, but all to come to repentance.[18]*

We live in this place, in the now, not because we have sinned and are being called back, but because this is where the prodigals who are being called back to the Kingdom of God are living, for

> *'Everyone who calls on the name of the Lord shall be saved.' But how are they to call on one in whom they have not believed? And how are they to believe in one of whom they have never heard? And how are they to hear without someone to proclaim him?[19]*

Indeed, any salvific process which whisked the redeemed off to a holy and perfect place would remove the living vehicle through whom the Lord chooses to reveal his salvation from the context in which the salvation is needed. Christians will enter the fullness of the Kingdom, but they cannot do so until the Lord returns. The work of which we ourselves are both recipient and participant is not yet complete[20], and it is in this place of need that the work of salvation is required.

---

[16] See Matthew 25.30, for example

[17] From Isaiah 11.6

[18] 2 Peter 3.9

[19] Romans 10.13-14

[20] See Philippians 1.6, for example. The word used there has the sense not only of completion, but of perfection, accomplishment, and ending. This completion is in God's hands.

In the Hebrew Scriptures we see exile as God's way of calling his people back to himself: God is faithful and blesses his people, they rebel, he sends them into exile in order that they might repent and return.

In the new covenant of Christ our primary citizenship and our first belonging are no longer limited to this created order. We are citizens of heaven[21], but we are called to live in this place, for this time, for the sake of the salvation of the world. God's people are called to follow the way of Jesus and live faithfully in exile in order that others might repent and return just as those who have already met Christ are privileged to have done.

Given this insight, there is much that we could learn from the biblical understanding of exile to help us live faithfully and fruitfully today. If this is a model which offers transferrable learning, and I am arguing that there is much in it that does, we must surely attend to the lessons it would offer.

So, let's turn our mind to deeper consideration and do the work I have just sketched out a bit more thoroughly. The prize is worth the effort, for we desperately need this. In the next chapter we will turn our mind to the Hebrew Scriptures and ask what lessons we might learn from the faithful in exile. In the remainder of this chapter we will explore four avenues that I have noticed we need to reflect upon in the New Testament. As we reflect upon them, I will seek to lay out some of the riches from this overlooked part of the biblical tradition as we look for wisdom to help us live in the now.

Exile in 1 Peter

The first arena we might explore is Peter's description of us as having citizenship in a kingdom different to the one we are living in, of us being a chosen race, a royal priesthood, a holy

---

[21] See Philippians 3.20 or Ephesians 2.19, for example

nation, God's own people[22]. He urges us as *'aliens and strangers in this world'* to abstain from the desires of the flesh, to conduct ourselves honourably *'among the Gentiles'*. This is language of a nation in exile. Indeed, the NRSV translates 'strangers' (παρεπιδήμους (parepidemos) – a resident foreigner) as 'exiles' (and while I am doing translation, let me point out the obvious truth that 'alien' (παροίκους (paroikos)) simply means one who is a resident foreigner, stranger, a dweller here from elsewhere (it doesn't mean 'a little green man from mars'); interestingly it is the word from which we get the English word 'parish' but this is for a different reason[23]).

1 Peter 2, where Peter uses this language, begins with an urgent call for Christians, who have tasted that the Lord is good, to live in a manner which is holy, and to come back to Christ. This is the very core of who we are in Christ, if indeed we are in Christ. Peter reminds us who we are, a chosen race, a royal priesthood, a holy nation, God's own people, and then urges us to live in a manner which sets us apart from those around us and points them to the One in whom we have found life and belonging. In particular we are instructed to *'accept the authority of every human institution... emperor or governor'* (13-14), and to honour everyone, especially the emperor (Peter seems to have a thing about the emperor). He then goes on to instruct slaves to accept the authority of their masters (which is a concept we return to in Book 3 as it is not without difficulty in the modern world[24]).

Consider the logic of the chapter:

---

[22] See 1 Peter 2.9ff

[23] The word parish comes from the same root, although actually via the Latin, and means 'those who dwell alongside or around': the community around a church building. I am biased as an Anglican, but one of the things I love about the way that we do church is that we are there for and with all who live in an area not only for the faithful. The parish church is literally meant to be the church for all who live around the household of faith rather than just being the household of faith.

[24] See Chapter 3 of *Dancing with Powerlessness*, Book 3 of this series

- Be holy so you might grow (1)
- Be hungry to grow into all God has for you (2-3)
- Come back to him and to each other and let him shape you together and for his glory (4-6)
- For Christ is all in all and those who do not see this will perish (7-8)
- But you are different, chosen, holy... (9a)
- ... so that you might proclaim God's mighty acts of salvation (9b-10)
- So be holy so you might witness (11-12a: note the repeated theme of holiness. This matters!)
- Submit to those in authority (13-14, 16b-20)
- Because your submission brings revelation from God to others (15)
- And this is what Christ did and it is what you are called to in grace (21-25)
- But it is not your eternal identity – you are free both now and then and for now are called to use that freedom in the Lord's service (16a)

In all of this, our forebears would have had to work out how to compromise. For example, if you are a slave and your master goes to worship at the temple, how to you square the circle of obedience to your master and to your Master? Or, as a citizen, how do you honour an emperor when that emperor declares himself to be a god and is treated as such? (The Caesars used to claim and be acclaimed as Lord. You see this on their coins, for example, where the inscription on a denarius reads *'Tiberivs Caesar Divi Avgvsti Filivs Avgvstvs'* ('Caesar Augustus Tiberius, son of the Divine Augustus').) The records we have of the interrogation of St Polycarp of Smyrna make it clear that this is a real issue for early Christians as he is asked *'what harm is there for you to say 'Caesar is Lord' and to perform the sacrifices...'*.

This is the world in which our early Christian brothers and sisters lived, and they are instructed to live with honour. Working this compromise through is really complex. They, and thus we, are a people belonging to one Kingdom, living in another for a particular purpose. We are a people in exile.

Jesus' Prayer in John 17

This sense of his followers being those who belong to one kingdom but living in another, is exactly how Jesus prays for us in John 17.14-15. Here we see Jesus interceding for us in the context of his forthcoming departure from this world. There is a notably stark contrast, at least in the terms that Jesus usually uses, between the things of this world and the things of the Father:

- He prays for us because we do not belong to the world just as he does not (v16), but he is not asking the Father to take us out of the world (v15).
- In verse 20 we see that he explicitly prays for *all* who will follow his word, not simply those with him at that moment. In so doing, he picks up an important principle from the Hebrew Scriptures: what God speaks to the community of faith he speaks in an eternal present[25]. What Jesus has prayed for his disciples, he is praying for us now; we can rest assured in and on his promise that he is in us and with us. We are one with him, and his desire is that we might be with him where he now is. We are in this place for now and with a purpose, but our destiny is to be with Christ

---

[25] In Deuteronomy 5, in which Moses is speaking to the people of Israel before they enter the promised land, he is clear that the covenant that God made was with those to whom he is currently speaking even though they had not been at Horeb: *'The Lord our God made a covenant with us at Horeb.' (v2)*

We have been told that the generation which was at Horeb will have passed away before the people are allowed to enter the promised land into which they are about to cross. When they object, though, at least in the way I imagine the gap between verses 2 and 3, Moses remakes his point: *'Not with our ancestors did the Lord make this covenant, but with us, who are all of us here alive today.'* (v3) and then repeats it in v4: *'The Lord spoke with you face to face at the mountain, out of the fire'*. What God has spoken, he is speaking. He speaks in the now to his people in an eternally present covenant of love.

where he is. It is no surprise when we feel the tension of this calling; it is not easy. We are 'in this world, but not of it' as the popular phrase expresses it.

Exile in the book of Hebrews

We have seen Peter using exile imagery as a framework for faithful discipleship. Jesus holds it in prayer before the Father. In a moment we will look at Paul and the way he engages with it in a particular context. I also want to note that it is one of the themes running through the book of Hebrews.

I am not sure that we often wrestle with the book of Hebrews beyond a few key passages. This might be because its tone and content feels somewhat different to the rest of the New Testament, but ignoring it is a shame. It is an important book offering distinctive contributions to our understanding of faith. The opening chapters draw us repeatedly and insistently to Christ, who is '*the radiance of God's glory and the exact representation of his being, sustaining all things by his powerful word.*' Through him he has '*spoken to us in these last days*' and who has '*provided purification for our sins [and] has sat down at the right hand of the majesty in heaven.*'[26]

It is no surprise that, once the introduction is over, the clear instruction of the unknown author of this letter is,

> *Therefore, holy brothers and sisters, who share in the heavenly calling, fix your thoughts on Jesus, whom we acknowledge as our apostle and high priest.*[27]

This is an important turning point in the book; the author has focussed on Christ, and now turns in verse 7 of chapter 3 to our response. He cites the people of Israel's rebellious response to Moses, which led to their time in the wilderness prior to entering the promised land. When you hear the word, when

---

[26] See Hebrews 1.2-3
[27] Hebrews 3.1 NIVUK

you hear Christ, the writer argues, do not be like them in their exilic wandering, '*see to it, brothers and sisters, that none of you has a sinful, unbelieving heart that turns away from the living God...*'[28] In chapter 4 the argument rests on the assertion that '*the promise of entering his rest still stands,*'[29] that Christ has done this work as our great high priest who has already ascended into heaven and that we can now '*approach the throne of grace with boldness, so that we may receive mercy and find grace to help in time of need.*'[30]

The argument is clear; we have been saved, and there is a clear promise that we will enter the promised rest, but we are not there yet. The letter seeks repeatedly to reassure that the work of Christ is sufficient, and to urge us to stay faithful. Christ is the new high priest[31], in the order of Melchizedek[32], whose blood is sufficient[33] and whose sacrifice is once for all[34]. Because of this we are to remain faithful[35], to persevere and '*hold unswervingly to the hope we profess*'[36], learning from the great examples of faith.[37]

> *Therefore, since we are surrounded by so great a cloud of witnesses, let us also lay aside every weight and the sin that clings so closely, and let us run with perseverance the race that is set before us, looking to Jesus the pioneer and perfecter of our faith, who for the sake of the joy that was set before him endured the cross, disregarding its shame, and has taken his seat at the right hand of the throne of God. Consider him who endured such hostility against himself from sinners, so that you may not grow weary or lose heart.*[38]

---

[28] Hebrews 3.12 NIVUK
[29] See Hebrews 4.1 or 4.6 for example.
[30] Hebrews 4.16
[31] Hebrews 5 and Hebrews 8
[32] Hebrews 7
[33] Hebrews 9
[34] Hebrews 10
[35] See the later parts of Hebrews 5
[36] Hebrews 10.23 NIVUK
[37] Hebrews 11
[38] Hebrews 12.1-3

This is not instruction being given to those who are outside the community of faith or who are rebellious against their Lord; this is teaching being given to the faithful about how they live in this place faithfully and receive it as the discipline and training of the Lord. This is how the book comes into land in chapters 12 and 13; we live in the now within the training and discipline of the Lord in order that we might be fruitful and bear a good harvest. We live in this exilic place, not because it is our promised rest, but because this is the place of our current calling so that God's work may be done.

> Do not, therefore, abandon that confidence of yours; it brings a great reward. For you need endurance, so that when you have done the will of God, you may receive what was promised.[39]

Exile in Romans 1

Most strikingly for me, though, I come back to Romans 1. This is a really important passage in which the apostle wrestles with the theme of judgement. It is not the easiest bit of the Bible to read, as Paul talks bluntly and engages with uncomfortable themes like the wrath of God. Thus, to our peril, we often ignore this teaching. I cannot actually think when I last heard someone preach on it. We have no substantive active popular theology which engages with the concept of a God of love who also knows wrath. It seems to me that we usually set love and wrath in opposition to each other and prefer to think only about God's love, despite the fact that this is not a consistent view of love.

Possibly the reason for this is an aversion to the kind of 'fire and brimstone' preaching which abides in popular memory in an almost mythical fashion (in that I am not sure most of us hear much of this week by week but somehow the memory persists). Such preaching can appear to portray our God as if he

---

[39] Hebrews 10.35-36

were one who basically hates humanity but abides us out of a sense of duty. His love is grudging, but his anger flows naturally. This, of course, is very far from the picture painted in the Bible or incarnated in Jesus Christ, and is not a view that any serious Christian teacher would, or should, espouse. However, the fact that *that* portrayal of God is false does not negate the existence in the scriptures of wrath, and we cannot edit this out. Moreover, I am not convinced that we should try. All love involves wrath, and the more intense the love the greater the wrath: we just need to look at where the wrath is directed and how it is acted upon.

I remember the first time I thought one of my kids was being bullied. The children involved were little more that toddlers, but something primal rose within me and a voice (albeit a controlled and instantly overruled voice) in my gut would have rained very real wrath down on the infantile persecutors' heads: I didn't want them so much as to frown at my little angel ever again. The fact that I didn't act in that way (as you can imagine, common sense and reasonableness easily prevailed and all was sorted out very amicably as part of the normal life of children in community) doesn't diminish the point: my wrath was a normal and healthy part of the dynamic of a father's love. It would not have been normal, right, or healthy were it the only emotion. It would not have been good to act on it, or to leave it unchecked or unbalanced. Wrath rightly sits within many other dynamics, and is rarely (if ever) a proper driving motivation for action in human relations, but it is there and real, and we are in dangerous waters if we overlook this. Love draws it out and it is powerful.

In Romans 1 we see the wrath of God being revealed against ungodliness and wickedness. It is not revealed against a person, but against actions and attitudes. Neither is it described in a manner which is violent when it comes to its revelation. Indeed, the action resulting from the revelation of wrath is remarkably gentle: God gives people up. He does not smite them, rather he does as they wish him to do. It is as if he says 'you wanted life without me; here it is...' and this is not the only place in the scriptures we see this dynamic spelled out. God respects the choice of his children to walk away from him, with the motivation that in leaving them to their own devices they might be called back to his way. Seeing this in the context of wrath might not be comfortable, but it is not the god of judgement that we sometimes fear it might be. Let's have a closer look at the chapter verse by verse, because it is really important to understand this:

- Verses 16-17 provide a really clear context: this is about the Gospel, Good News. Paul is talking about salvation which is available to all whether Jew or Gentile. This is powerful stuff which is effective in the now, and in it God's righteousness will be found and inhabited.

- Verse 18 jumps, in what seems to the modern reader to be quite a dramatic way, straight to the concept that the wrath of God is being revealed against the wickedness displayed by the suppression of God's truth.
  It begins with the word 'for', clearly linking this to the previous line of thought: this is the result of the righteousness of God into which Christians are liberated by the Good News that has been preached. The logic is clear though:
  ○ God is righteous and calls his children to righteousness,
  ○ the world is not righteous, and
  ○ this results at one and the same time both in God's displeasure and in the freedom offered in the gospel (as set out in the previous verses).

- These things should not come as a surprise, Paul argues in verses 19 onwards. 'Look around you', he seems to say. You can see everything you need to know about God through his work of creation; his kindness, his glory, his power, his presence. These have meant that we have seen and understood God even though he remains invisible to us.

- Despite these clearly visible facts, Paul argues in verse 21 people neither gave God honour or lived in gratitude to him which leads to futile thinking and darkened minds. There is something really important here about a diagnosis of human isolation from God. When we choose to live outside a spiritual dynamic of praise and thankfulness life will run into the sand. Philosophy becomes a dead end, and action becomes worthless.
  Life is empty without the creator at the centre, and the embrace with which we cling to the Father's love is held and shaped by encircling arms of praise and gratitude.

- As a result of people's choices God has given humanity over, or up, to the consequences of their repeated and settled choice about the way they live. This can be in no doubt because the same word[40] is repeated three times (in verses 24, 26, and 28).

- In verse 24 we are given up to impurity and the degrading of our bodies in lust because we worship the created rather than the Creator

- In verse 26 we are given up to degrading passions, inappropriate sexual acts, and we receive due penalty

- And in verse 28 we are given up to a debased mind and inappropriate action: ruthlessness, heartlessness, foolishness and faithlessness, jealously, insolence, arrogant boasting, gossip, slander, evildoers who invent yet more evil, murderers, and those who rebel against their parents.

- It is important to note two things about the way that this is expressed.
  - It is not that God leads humanity to this place, rather that he sees that this is where we have chosen to go and gives us over to it. This is consequence not judgement; judgement is withheld, and for now we

---

[40] παραδίδωμι: 'given over' see page 43

are given over to a place of darkness and depravity in order that the power and invitation of the Gospel might be made plain.

○ God has given humanity over, not merely some humans. I think many English translations are unhelpful here as they imply that there are *some* humans against whom the wrath of God is being revealed and who are given over. The sense of the passage, though, is more that because humanity *as a whole* has made this choice we are *all* given over. This is made even more clear in the first verses of Romans 2, to which we return below, and is consonant with the rest of Paul's writings and with the flow of the scriptures. We find ourselves captive to the 'things of this world' and yet yearning for Christ. We live in a place of exile as we have been set in this context, and our salvation is drawing us out into the things of God in a manner which is not yet fully realised.

Listen to the apostle himself, writing later in the same book:

> *'...we know that the law is spiritual; but I am of the flesh, sold into slavery under sin. I do not understand my own actions. For I do not do what I want, but I do the very thing I hate. Now if I do what I do not want, I agree that the law is good. But in fact it is no longer I that do it, but sin that dwells within me. For I know that nothing good dwells within me, that is, in my flesh. I can will what is right, but I cannot do it. For I do not do the good I want, but the evil I do not want is what I do. Now if I do what I do not want, it is no longer I that do it, but sin that dwells within me.*
>
> *So I find it to be a law that when I want to do what is good, evil lies close at hand. For I delight in the law of God in my inmost self, but I see in my members another law at war with the law of my mind, making me captive to the law of sin that dwells in my members. Wretched man that I am! Who will rescue me from this body of death? Thanks*

> *be to God through Jesus Christ our Lord!*
> *So then, with my mind I am a slave to the*
> *law of God, but with my flesh I am a slave*
> *to the law of sin.*[41]

We who follow Christ do not stand apart from those who are given over; we are among them and distinguished only in that we are being saved from the consequences of our shared rebellion. We are in exile, but we are headed home.

- And lest there be any doubt that this applies to us too, Romans 2 carries straight on *'Therefore you have no excuse, whoever you are, when you judge others; for in passing judgement on another you condemn yourself, because you, the judge, are doing the very same things.*[42] Remember that there is no break in the Greek manuscript, chapter breaks are a later insertion. What Paul writes at the end of Romans 1 is not simply some constitution for a holy club where members can pass judgement on naughty people within society; it is an analysis of the state of humanity; that we are given over to the choices we have made by a God who loves us so much that he will not force himself upon us. And this is where we find ourselves as Christians; hunkered in the now, longing for the not-yet.

Exile as integral to the New Covenant

In these four different examples we see this concept worked out: we really are a people in exile for now. We live in a place which is not ultimately home, among a people to whom we do not primarily belong, and seek to be faithful to a God who is imminent and yet outwith the society we inhabit. And yet we are not abandoned, we are not hopeless, and we are called to live as a wise people with the grace of holy exiles. We are a

---

[41] Romans 7.14-25
[42] Romans 2.1

prophetic community who will be tried and tested even as we are called home and held in salvation grace. Again, we see this throughout the New Testament, but let's consider the examples we have been looking at in this chapter.

In 1 Peter 2 we have noted the call to live holy lives. All of this is set in the context, though, of tasting that the Lord is good and being invited to come to him. We have received mercy. We are invited to consent to being built into a spiritual house, or a holy priesthood in order that our sacrifices might be found acceptable. It is in this context that Peter explains, and then re-emphasises that we are a holy people, God's people. We weren't, but now we are. Interestingly there are two things he repeats in this chapter: our call to honour *both* the emperor *and* our nature as the people of God. We are a holy people and we are called to live in this desperately uncomfortable compromise in the now. Holiness does not require, indeed cannot thrive in, separation. We are aliens but we are not abandoned.

This is the whole point of the book of Hebrews. The book seems to shout the question in every chapter: how do you live faithfully in exile? Look at our history! Look at Christ! God has not given up on you and the promised rest is still promised. Be faithful and we will always find that the Lord is more faithful.

Or think back to John 17 where we see the same dynamic in the praying of our Lord. As we have seen he does not ask for us to be removed from the world, but he does ask for us to be protected (11 &15), sanctified (17), and united (21, 22, 23) in order that the world may believe (21, 23). We are not abandoned or disowned, but we are called to be here and to be here for a purpose. Once again, we see that our exile is purposeful both internally (in our own discipleship) and externally (in mission and witness), and that the external focus seems key. We are here to complete the missional work of Christ and we do that by living in the place of exile in order that others may come to believe.

We see this most clearly in Romans. I have already set out that we live in a state of 'given-over-ness' with our fellow humans, and this is set out three times in five verses with the repeated use of the word παραδίδωμι (paradidomi, which is simply the specific word used for 'given over'). What is striking, though, in the context of the whole book of Romans is that we are not alone in this. Later Paul will write that

> [Jesus] was handed over (παραδίδωμι) to death for our trespasses and was raised for our justification[43]

Jesus, in his incarnation, joins us in this exilic place and is given over by the Father just as we have been. We may be in a place of exile for the purpose of mission, but we are not alone in this place and it is not our mission alone. This is emphasised and repeated later,

> He who did not withhold his own Son, but gave him up (παραδίδωμι) for all of us, will he not with him also give us everything else?[44]

Here we find ourselves called to, and participating in, the very work of the heart of God... this reaching out to all his children that all may hear and all may be given the chance to hear and respond, to 'come to their senses'[45] and realise that life really is better around the Father's table in that place that really is home.

Conclusion

Exile is an integral part of the work of God, but as I said when I introduced the term, I do need to reiterate that I am using a common word in an uncommon way. I am using the language of exile and applying it to the new-covenant people of God. Much of the language of exile in the Hebrew Scriptures arises

---

[43] Romans 4.25
[44] Romans 8.32
[45] To borrow a term used of the younger, or prodigal, son in Luke 15.

in the context of the sin of Israel. The crude narrative of Jewish history is that God gives them the security of the promised land, but when they sin he sends them to captivity and exile to call them back to himself. In these exilic places he raises up the faithful who witness to his way, and through them the voice of truth and hope is heard. Post Christ, this picture is a little different. I am arguing that we are living in exile for the sake of the sin of the created order, just as Christ did, not merely for our own sinfulness and redemption. We, of course, share in the sin of the created order unlike him, but we also share in his work. This has always been true, but in the relative luxury of a 'Christendom' era, it seems that it is quite possible to forget it.

I re-stress the point as we come to the end of this chapter. Whilst it might feel like slightly odd language, there is much vital wisdom that we can learn from this part of the biblical corpus and Christian tradition. We turn our mind to some examples of this wisdom. What can we learn, both positively and negatively, from the experience of exile as we seek to live faithfully and fruitfully today?

We follow the pattern of *Clinging to the Cross* (Book 1 of this series), and begin by considering some potential pitfalls with this metaphor. Please note, though, that we look at the challenges in order that we might then more fully inhabit the rich offering of grace and hope that the Bible offers through this major theme. If chapter 3 begins to weigh you down, do turn straight on to chapter 4!

2A - PAUSING FOR BREATH

Pause for a moment and consider. What issues are you wrestling with that have caused you to pick up this book? If the following questions are useful, please use them to reflect:

1) What have I noticed the Spirit of God saying to me in this chapter?
   a) What have I learned?
   b) Where do I want to reflect further?
   c) What ideas will not go away?
2) In what ways does it make sense of Christian life to think of it as exilic, as we wait for Christ's return?
3) How do we walk alongside sisters and brothers in Christ if we are supporting each other in exile?
4) What do I need to do in response to what God is saying to me?

3 - DEVALUING EXILE

Exile, then, is a key theme for us to inhabit if we are to follow Christ faithfully in our modern world. It is, though, relatively unfamiliar to most of us (at least in the terms that I am using it). This is, I think, the opposite of the problems that we sometimes have with the cross which we explored in chapter 3 of *Clinging to the Cross* (Book 1 in this series[46]) where we are so familiar with the language of the cross that we can almost treat it with contempt. With exile, perhaps the danger is more that we could come across a new way of thinking about a theme which we may never have applied to ourselves and shoot off in directions that we later need to rethink.

In this chapter (in a similar way to our consideration of how we might respond unhelpfully to thinking around the cross) we pause and notice some of the cautions we might bear in mind. I am nervous, I confess, though, about the second half of this chapter as it could be taken out of context and misused. I don't want to write people (or their views) off, point fingers, or pick arguments. I simply want to help us notice where we might wander off in unintended directions. Mostly I want to open the Bible to those who have to wrestle to be faithful in complex, uncertain, and changing circumstances. I have a really high confidence in the scriptures, and want people to read them. It changes everything.

Once again, then, I have a basic observation and then some subjective reflections. Please feel free to add copiously to the latter (as with all that I offer, I hope that this is a springboard to your own reflections, thoughts, and insight).

---

[46] Details of the book available at little-house-in-joppa.uk/home

Assuming we recognise this basic concept of new-covenant exile, it seems to me that there are four basic ways we could respond in an unhealthy manner.

1. We can refute the idea of exile completely, because we choose to assert that God's reign is already here.
2. We can realise we are in exile in theory, but choose to club together so closely with other Christians that we cut ourselves off from those who have not yet realised the offer of a greater citizenship in Christ and live as if we aren't exiled at all.
3. We can realise we are in exile and simply assimilate.
4. We can reject any learning from the idea of exile, or at least exilic faithfulness, because we don't believe God has any power anyway.

I hope that I have already established why the first and final problems would be worrying. Denial of a problem does not usually remove the problem. Indeed, it can often compound the problem by lulling us into a sense of security whilst we have the capacity to address the issue and then leaving us stranded when we are beset by its ramifications.

The middle two, though, concern me just as much. Living in isolation or assimilation may appear to be effective survival strategies, but both disable the very purpose of the exile into which we are saved, sent, and secured. We may neither claim ontological insecurity as holiness, nor pragmatic assimilation as missional relevance: rather we are called to a deeply secure rootedness in Christ which enables us to inhabit our identity as engaged exile in a world which will always remain alien.[47]

This, though, is my key observation: both of the middle two options seem attractive, and I wonder if this is partly because we crave certainty (especially in uncertain exilic times). By way of silly example, I was thinking about emoji (or 'emojis', which is an alternative plural and wryly illustrates the point I am about to make) which various of my friends tease me about. My usage

---

[47] I am referring back to 1 Peter 2.11, in case the language seems strange

is, apparently, idiosyncratic and it is made all the more so by a lack of clarity about exactly what an emoji means. This is the point of them, of course, but it is embarrassing when you send a picture of a vegetable or piece of fruit and discover you have sent a suggestive message without realising. Apparently 😅 is a useful emoji 'because it has a variety of meanings', but it leaves me concerned that I might send you a message which I mean as kind and you receive as insult. It is a world with rules I know I do not fully know, and leaves me either wanting not to use emojis at all or to define each one before I use it. In exile (and in messaging) we cannot do this: we cannot either withdraw permanently from the place of exile if this is where God is sending us, nor can we simply assimilate as *'if salt has lost its saltiness, how can you season it?'[48]*

Exile involves uncertainty. We cannot, we must not remove this. It is uncomfortable at times, but it is also an adventure, literally an adventure of faith.

Biblical corrections of exile

One way we can reflect on this is to consider teaching by which the Bible corrects the behaviour of those who are in exile. What guidance do we see?

Exiles pray for the wellbeing of the city

To start with, exiles are to be a people of blessing not of curse. We have alluded to Daniel in the reflection that started this section, and will explore below (see pages 92 and 98) something of how he and his companions served and did so

---

[48] To quote Jesus in Mark 9.50: Jesus' point here is that we are called to be salt in the earth, and we are not able to be that if we lose the very thing that makes us effective, that makes us 'salt'. You probably know but 'salt' in the ancient world was not pure, containing various sandy constituents. Thus 'salt' could easily lose its saltiness in a manner that does not quite makes sense to our modern minds.

honourably. I think of Jeremiah's explicit teaching, instructing *'you must not listen to your prophets, your diviners, your dreamers, your soothsayers, or your sorcerers, who are saying to you, 'You shall not serve the king of Babylon.' For they are prophesying a lie to you, with the result that you will be removed far from your land; [the LORD] will drive you out, and you will perish'.*[49] The same warning is repeated a few verses later in very similar words. Rather the faithful are to *'seek the welfare of the city where I have sent you into exile, and pray to the Lord on its behalf, for in its welfare you will find your welfare.'*[50]

This is true practically: Christians are not called away from their civic and societal responsibilities in a nation. We are instructed to be model citizens. More than this: it is true 'spiritually', and this is the main point I am making here. Exile is part of our spiritual life and worship not separate from it.

Exiles turn from the worship of Baal

At the same time, we are not to worship the 'gods' that are worshipped around us. One of my favourite stories in the Bible is found in 1 Kings 18.20-39, where we see Elijah dramatically making this point: Israel must be faithful to the one true God. Our belonging in a place does not dethrone God in our lives.

Exile engages the whole person and is transformative

One of the obvious places to turn in the scriptures when thinking through this question is Romans 12.1-2:

> *I appeal to you therefore, brothers and sisters, by the mercies of God, to present your bodies as a living sacrifice, holy and acceptable to God, which is your spiritual worship. Do not be conformed to this world, but be transformed by the renewing of your minds, so that you may discern what is the will of God—what is good and acceptable and perfect.*

---

[49] Jeremiah 27.9-10
[50] Jeremiah 29.7

There are two things that leap out at me almost every time I come back to these verses. The first is the delightful interplay of body and mind. As we follow the Christ who calls us to love God with all our heart, soul, mind and strength this should not be a surprise, but please do notice that faithful inhabiting of exile will be whole-person discipleship.

Secondly, there is this clear call to be transformed (which is an ongoing call in the specific sense of the words used in text – 'go on being transformed' rather than 'go and get yourself transformed and then come back ready for the next thing'). This transformation is neither conformity with the patterns of this world, nor is it withdrawal from the world. It is an invitation deeper and deeper into the image of God.

Thirdly, it is engaged transformation for the purpose of keeping in step with the will of God. This means that it is about mission, worship, discipleship, witness, and so on. This is exactly the call that we are discussing: a call into the mission of God.

I could go on giving examples. I think of the teaching of the prophets (that, if God sends us to exile it is only there that we can meet him[51]), instructions to slaves (to serve faithfully even if their masters are not Christians (and there are many issues here, I realise)[52]), or to each of us to pray for those in authority.[53]

What I want to do in the rest of this chapter, though, is to reflect a bit on how we read the Bible in exile. There is a deep parallel

---

[51] See Micah 4.10, for example
[52] See Ephesians 6.5-8 '*Slaves, obey your earthly masters with fear and trembling, in singleness of heart, as you obey Christ; not only while being watched, and in order to please them, but as slaves of Christ, doing the will of God from the heart. Render service with enthusiasm, as to the Lord and not to men and women, knowing that whatever good we do, we will receive the same again from the Lord, whether we are slaves or free.*' This is not a hook that Paul wants to let us wriggle off.
[53] See Romans 13.1-7, for one example.

here between a constructive approach to the scriptures and a healthy approach to this second-covenant-exilic living. The temptation is always to hold the scriptures either too tightly or too loosely, to demand that they say everything or say nothing. In exile we can choose either to lose ourselves uncritically with those around us or to withdraw as if we need to be afraid. This can, at times, lead to an oddly divided existence where we define ourselves tightly in some parts of life by what we think the Bible says, and at other times by the world's values[54]. It can mean that we identify only with our favoured 'tribe' of exiles and allow their views to define our view on everything (whether or not the Bible speaks about it).

Life can, though, be more than either of these extremes if we will be learn to dance humbly in the middle space, and exile is the dance-floor. Faithful living in exile takes great care and huge humility. Being cut off from the temple requires engagement, improvisation, and the hiding of God's word deep in the heart[55]. The Bible itself, it seems to me, refuses to be constrained by our exile (in fact it is often liberated by in unexpected ways in such contexts): it is living and active[56] and will continue to speak in its own, indeed in God's, voice until we will listen.

The glorious realism of the Bible

You will have noticed that I keep coming back to the Bible. I do so because it matters, but I notice that each of us can live in a particular kind of fear of the Bible, even though our fears might be different. Some live with fear that it is a harsh and judgemental book which will simply condemn them. Others

---

[54] Just a couple of weeks ago I was talking with someone who held a traditional view on homosexuality, but was completely open to transsexuality 'because the Bible doesn't say anything about that'. I desperately wanted to ask how far this went, but was very restrained.

[55] See Psalm 119.11

[56] See Hebrews 4.12

fear that those who read it openly have changed their minds on slavery, divorce, or women in ministry so now we will do the same with sex (or whatever the current issue we are facing might be), and become ever more strident in their holding of the text in a particular manner. Reading fearfully is not a very good sign when it comes to the biblical text, though, and I find I need to challenge both fears, at least within myself. We simply cannot bury our collective head in sand and pretend there are no tricky issues in the Bible and thus avoid the challenges. More than that, though, when we approach the scriptures with fear we miss the riches that are there for the harvesting. We treat a feast as if it were a trap, a love-letter as if it were a test, and the best-ever news as if it were merely an advert designed to mislead.

This is where the nervousness I mentioned earlier come in. It is so easy to see the Bible as harsh and unbending when we face new circumstances or realise there is more to understand than we had grasped in our missional context. The experience of the faithful through the ages, though, is that there are depths and riches for every circumstance in the scriptures that are bigger, kinder, deeper, and more inviting than we have yet realised. I want to point to some of these here to invite you to bring your real wrestling into conversation with the text. I am not arguing for any standpoint, simply opening our eyes to the richness of our inheritance. Nevertheless I fear this will not be read this way, and make the point partly to invite you to look deeper if the way I write makes you feel this way.

The Bible is the most gloriously real book ever written. I cannot think that there are any issues at all that it ducks, from things that we might secretly enjoy reading about (be they innuendo, baldness, or greed) or things that break our hearts (like incest, bitterness, or genocide). In all of this we glimpse a God who is far bigger, far more robust, far more loving, and far more real than we have even begun to be. It is not a book of easy answers; it is a book, THE book, of life – real life – life wrought through the Son, lived in the Spirit, to the glory of the Father. We must never domesticate or bridle it, particularly as preachers and teachers. Our task is to open the text and invite people in; to inhabit the narrative and offer people real hope. In saying this I am not pushing in one direction or another, I am challenging you, dear reader, to inhabit the confidence that rightly belongs in the scriptures.

Be careful of overly-easy answers

Two jokes featuring a Sunday-School teacher asking a question come to mind. Both are old, I am afraid, and neither is particularly funny, but each makes an interesting point. In the first, the teacher asks *'what is grey, with a fluffy tail, lives in trees, and eats nuts?'* and a child replies, *'well, it sounds like a squirrel to me, but I know that the answer must be Jesus.'* In the second, which plays even more on stereo-types in a manner I find slightly offensive (although it was first told to me by a friend who is a Rabbi, so maybe I am being over-sensitive), we see a young boy of Jewish heritage who has been parked in Sunday School so his parents can get a morning's peace. The teacher explains that there is a prize, and asks who the most important leader in the Bible is. When the boy answers *'Jesus'*, he is asked why he didn't think it was Moses or Abraham. *'Religion is religion'*, he replies, *'but business is business'*.

These jokes (and I did warn you that neither was funny) highlight the twin dangers of easy answers or functionalism when it comes to the Bible. Neither mindless simplicity nor unreflective pragmatism will do.

We can adopt some fairly awful tendencies when we come to addressing tricky questions around matters of faith. We assume that the answers are staring us in the face and either step back from our deeper searching out of a desire to conform with those around us or withdraw with the assumption that we are going to be judged. The Bible simply doesn't do this, preferring instead a deeply raw engagement with reality. It takes courage and remarkable vulnerability to remain open to ongoing wrestling with faith. So much courage, in fact, that I fear we assume that we have heard before we listen; that we know what the text or other people are going to say, and even what they think, before we take time to hear what they are trying to communicate. Personally, I do believe that, at a profound level, Jesus is the answer to the deepest and most vital questions. However, this answer is rarely easy, or straightforward, and usually leads to deeper wrestling as God draws us *'come further up, come further in'*.[57] Truth is embodied in a person and a relationship; it is not some magic formula to wave away difficult issues.

Moreover, whilst the scriptures are very clear on the core issues and deeply challenging to all of us in a profound call to repentance[58] and the reshaping of life, there are some questions it is difficult to answer simply, not least because the Bible itself doesn't answer them simply. Sometimes, perhaps, we would be wise to recognise this rather more openly than we do. Contrary to the defensive myths of adolescent Christianity, at least in my experience of it, acknowledging that there are areas of uncertainty does not remove our assurance about the things we know clearly. Indeed, I would argue it rather strengthens them both now and in the long-term. For example, we know that there is only one unforgivable sin, namely that of blaspheming against the Holy Spirit. As Jesus says *"Truly I tell you, people will be forgiven for their sins and whatever blasphemies they utter; but whoever blasphemes against the Holy Spirit can never have forgiveness, but is guilty of an eternal sin'*.[59] This much is clear: all can be forgiven but this one thing… and yet we are not clear what comprises blasphemy against the Holy Spirit.

So what do we do? Do we ignore the problem, forget it, or pretend it doesn't exist? Often, perhaps we do, but this is really

---

[57] This, lest the reader is intrigued, is a reference back to CS Lewis' 'The Last Battle'

[58] See note on page 60

[59] Mark 3.28-29 paralleled in Matthew 12.31-32 and Luke 12.10. This is not something which appears once and can be swept aside as a minor thought.

dangerous. Where we insist on certainty that goes beyond the text, we might be able to live with the myth of clarity for a time, but at some point we will face the fact that we have created a false foundation and the real danger is that we will throw the whole of our faith away on the basis that we had trusted some partial assumptions. The call to the faithful is far deeper and more lasting than this; as we engage with the scriptures we are invited to hold them open handed, to allow them to breathe, to speak, to fight back, to be willing to wrestle with them as Jacob wrestled with God. To use more domestic and agricultural image, we are to live with them whether or not we find them easy, we are to chew them like a cow chewing the cud. We chew things over, and leave them for a while (a cow has several stomachs for this), and then chew them some more because digestion takes time when you are eating tough stuff. We recognise that understanding takes time, and importantly that it always leaves us changed. Wrestling with God left Jacob walking with a limp for the rest of his life.

A note about repentance (which is too big for a footnote):

I note, in passing, that I am less and less sure that we are clear about what we mean by repentance. We can assume it is merely a deep expression of regret and apology, not least because that understanding almost makes sense of the biblical text. However, it doesn't fully do so and we do need to think more deeply.

Think of Mark 1.4 and Mark 1.15 where we see both John the Baptist and Jesus call people to repentance. It could be that both are simply inviting people to express how bad they have been and that they now regret it. This is the way such passages are usually preached. The required response to such a call is 'I am a bad person, I see that, I want to be new, and I come to Christ.' As I say, there is some truth to this view, but there are a number of problems with this meaning, including:

1. It is not what the word 'repent' actually means: the best translation of the word is more like 'be(ing) of new/other mind/understanding'. This repentance does involve a leaving behind of old understanding and will contain sorrow, but the emphasis is on the new way of grasping reality. We get this wrong when we say repentance means turning around (it just doesn't!). Of course there is a sense of turning our backs on the old way of living, but we do so because there is an utter transformation of our whole life: a new understanding, a new conception, a new realisation, a new hope, a new freedom. This is the joy of repentance!

2. It implies that repentance only involves laying down the bad bits of our lives, whereas in reality coming to Christ involves bringing all that we are and finding ourselves daily transformed by his amazing goodness. He transforms our brokenness and also transforms the stuff we think is sorted, good, and strong. Repentance in its true sense involves offering all this to Him.

It fails to capture the meaning of repentance in the Bible. Think of Jeremiah 18.1-11 where some translations talk of God changing his mind and others talk of God repenting. The words for God's 'repentance' and ours are different (both in Hebrew and in the Greek translation available to the writers of the New Testament), but the parallelism is clear. We repent, God repents. God does not need to lay down the wrong or bad bits of his life, rather he changes his actions based on the choices made by humankind. He steps into a new reality which is, in part, defined by the choice that we make, and more fully defined by his own goodness with a constant bias to blessing wherever possible. This is repentance.

Reading in (Christian) faith

Let me illustrate with a perspective from beyond our faith. One of the privileges I have had in my working life is to engage with Jewish and Islamic leaders in a process called Scriptural Reasoning. It is basically like Bible study, except that each person brings a passage from their own scriptures and the whole group discusses it. It is unceasingly interesting to discuss passages from the Hebrew Scriptures with Jewish friends and engage both with their understanding and their methodology of study. As a Christian in this three-way process, it is interesting to come to the Qur'anic passages because both the Jewish and the Christian Scriptures comprise the Bible for me, but the Qur'an sits outwith this, both in content and methodology. And, indeed, we non-Islamic hearers are already stretching Muslim practice by hearing the Qur'an in English given our lack of Arabic. On one occasion we heard a reading which described the earliest encounter between David and Bathsheba. Both Jews and Christians in the group were astonished to hear our Muslim friend explain that David did not sin despite the evidence of the text which seemed to be clear that he did. For a Muslim, it is a faith position that the five great prophets of Islam are sinless, and the text must be interpreted in this manner, we were told. *'How, then,'* I asked, *'do you understand the Qur'anic text?'*, and my friend said something I will never forget. *'We believe that a third of the Qur'an belongs to the people, a third to the scholars, and a third to the prophet alone.'* There are some bits, he explained, which faithful Muslims will never understand and simply accept.

This is markedly different to a Christian (and, actually, a Jewish) engagement with the Bible, and you could tell that by the mood of surprise in the room. As inquisitive Judeo-Christian, post-enlightenment others we were uncomfortable with our friend's response. We wrestle. We probe. We find ourselves convicted and liberated, and invited into more. We debate, and argue, and quest, and seek (and as Christians we believe that in seeking we find); in asking we receive, and in knocking we will someday find that the door is opened. But let's not pretend that this means every question is easy.

At the risk of being taken out of context, or being heard to say more than I am actually saying, let me give some examples.

What about eunuchs

Perhaps another example of wrestling with this gritty reality would be to ask what Jesus means when he says *'there are eunuchs who have been so from birth, and there are eunuchs who have been made eunuchs by others, and there are eunuchs who have made themselves eunuchs for the sake of the kingdom of heaven.'*[60] And how does this fit with the traditional Christian understanding that we are created male and female?[61] Clearly in context this teaching is about marriage, but is this all? In the conversation that gives rise to this statement, the disciples are shocked that Jesus teaches that divorce and remarriage is adultery, and observe that it would be better not to marry. This may be the context, but it is an odd way to say it to modern ears (I think we hear the word 'eunuch' simply to mean a castrated male). This verse has courted much argument, of course, and I am not going to solve it here. I observe that the literal meaning of εὐνοῦχος (eunochos) is 'I have the bed' or 'alone in bed', rather than something specifically to do with a lack of genitalia, but I suspect this is academic. It certainly reinforces the view that this verse could purely be metaphorical, and this is further supported by the teaching that some have made themselves eunuchs for the Kingdom of God; I don't know of many in our history who have chosen the path of castration as an act of devotion. However, the fact that Jesus observes that some are born eunuchs and others are made eunuchs does seem to imply that there are those who at the very least are outwith the 'normal' pattern of sexual activity.

---

[60] Matthew 19.12
[61] This is affirmed by Jesus earlier in the same discourse, see Matthew 19.4.

Does this imply that, within the biblical corpus, there are those whose sexual or gender identity sits beyond the normative biblical pattern of heterosexual procreative activity? I think the truth (and this is uncomfortable for each of us, whatever our own view) is that we do not know, but we would be unwise either to ignore millennia of Christian teaching or to ignore the fact that many who are asexual or of other gender identity see an echo of their experience in this verse... not least because the text, as we have received it, makes space for such self-understanding.

Some would say that they have been born in a body which does not fit with the gender they have been given, either in a binary sense of a man being born in a woman's body or in a bigger contemporary perception of the multiplicity of gender identity. Does the Bible allow for such a possibility? Might the fall and the resultant dislocation of the created order be such that the creation ordinance of male and female is shattered in such a manner? Few have suggested so until recent years and it is hard to construct a directly derivative biblical argument in this direction, but it is not impossible that this sits within a faithful holding of the canon.

What about divorce?

Or think about the question of divorce. In the passage with which we have just been wrestling we see two different orthodox patterns; one given by Moses and the other by Jesus. Of course, Jesus' teaching completes and perfects that of Moses, but it doesn't remove it from scripture. Moses permitted divorce, Jesus brings us back to the first teaching of the Bible, but even here there is an exception given: *'whoever divorces his wife, except for unchastity, and marries another commits adultery.'*[62] Divorce has no effect, unless there is infidelity, we are taught. Then, however, St Paul weighs in. He teaches:

---

[62] Matthew 12.9

> To the married I give this command—not I but the Lord—that
> the wife should not separate from her husband (but if she does
> separate, let her remain unmarried or else be reconciled to her
> husband), and that the husband should not divorce his wife.
>
> To the rest I say—I and not the Lord—that if any believer has
> a wife who is an unbeliever, and she consents to live with him,
> he should not divorce her. And if any woman has a husband
> who is an unbeliever, and he consents to live with her, she
> should not divorce him. For the unbelieving husband is made
> holy through his wife, and the unbelieving wife is made holy
> through her husband. Otherwise, your children would be
> unclean, but as it is, they are holy. But if the unbelieving
> partner separates, let it be so; in such a case the brother or
> sister is not bound. It is to peace that God has called you. [63]

There are so many interesting things in this passage. Paul
clearly applies his own judgement alongside the teaching that
he derives from the scriptures. He reinforces that there should
be no divorce, although permits that separation is permissible
on the condition that the partners remain single, in effect
married but apart. However, he then shimmies into his own
reflection in verse 12, stressing that this is his teaching and not
the Lord's, to instruct that divorce is permissible if an
unbelieving partner wishes to divorce a believer. The believer
is 'not bound' in this instance. There is much that we need to
understand if we are to live within this teaching as it is given.
Does the fact that the believing partner is not bound free them
to marry again, or are they constrained by the injunction to
singleness from the previous pericope, for example? Again, we
do not know for certain, but what we do know is that the
Apostle was applying his own teaching alongside that of Christ.

What about domestic violence?

So, what are we to do, theologically, in the case of domestic
violence? I hope no-one would defend or advocate the practice
of requiring an abused wife or husband to remain with their

---

[63] 1 Corinthians 7.10-15

spouse; such teaching would, in every situation I can see, be complicit with the abuse itself and very dangerous. In no sense am I promoting such coercion in exploring the question and I am ashamed to recognise that some have promulgated this view. The problem, theologically though, is that abuse is not mentioned either by Jesus or by Paul. Does this mean that a believing victim faces the choice between being the complicit recipient of abuse or committing a sin of their own in leaving? And what if there are children who are also subject to the violence of a mother or father?

Surely every thinking and compassionate Christian who wrestles with biblical ethics in the real world would advocate removing the children and the spouse from such a situation, and would not see this as contrary to the teaching of the Bible. There are differing opinions about whether such a refuge-seeking partner is free to divorce and remarry, or whether they are bound by marriage vows to a life of chastity. However, when you bring children into the picture this becomes more complicated again. Which is the greater good, the raising of children with no male or female parental role-model, or the fidelity of a spouse (through the choice of celibacy in this instance) to their abusive marital partner? People would advocate both, of course; I simply observe that it is a question on which there is variety in faithful interpretations of the scripture and our tradition. It is a question which highlights the truth that we come to scripture with minds and hearts engaged in the world around us.

Intelligently embracing disagreement

Moreover, we should neither assume that those with 'modern' answers to these questions have abandoned our shared historic teaching, nor that those with 'traditional' views have turned aside from the need for deep grace (or whatever characterising we might be tempted to do). Those who are ethically libertarian still need to practice deep penitence just as those who hold traditional lines must always do so with compassion. Neither approach (or any of the myriad or approaches that accompany them) permits us to loose our grasp on the call to love one another or to love God; it is in this split call that we find our identity and in which we offer sacrifice of praise.[64] Indeed, I would argue that this is our flawed but faithful worship. Think of the words of St Paul to the church in Rome:

> *I appeal to you therefore, brothers and sisters, by the mercies of God, to present your bodies as a living sacrifice, holy and acceptable to God, which is your spiritual worship. Do not be conformed to this world, but be transformed by the renewing of your minds, so that you may discern what is the will of God—what is good and acceptable and perfect.[65]*

We often think of Paul's words here as outward facing, which they clearly are, but they are also demonstrably based on an inward and upward focussed lively discipline of holy engagement. This passage follows Romans 11 in which Paul has been wrestling with God's ongoing work of salvation both for Jew and Gentile. God has not finished yet, and, of course, we are part of this work of mission, proclaiming the word and works of God, inviting all back into the loving embrace of God.

> *Just as you were once disobedient to God but have now received mercy because of their disobedience, so they have now been disobedient in order that, by the mercy shown to you, they too may now receive mercy. For God has imprisoned all in disobedience so that he may be merciful to all.[66]*

The call to the disciple is to a physical, bodily obedience which does not conform to the world. Why would a disciple have been tempted to conform to the world if they were not utterly immersed in the world? This teaching, once again, rests on the assumption that we are *in the world but not of it*. In this place, set in a missional context, we are to *be transformed by the renewal of our minds*, we are to think. We are to think hard, we

---

[64] See chapter 2 of *Clinging to the Cross* for a fuller discussion of this idea
[65] Romans 12.1-2
[66] Romans 11.30-32

are to think clearly, and this is to transform us in order that we might *discern what the will of God is*; in order that we might come to see what is *good, acceptable, and perfect* and live in accordance with it.

Please notice this! It is foundational and profound. Why does the apostle instruct us to think? Surely it is because things are not straightforward and we need to 'use our noggin' (as my granny used to say)? I have given examples of this already (concerning divorce, violence, and eunuchs) and I am about to give more. When we live with the assumption that faithfulness is merely simple obedience we are being overly childish (as opposed to child-like); being faithful is sometimes very complex.

The Christian view on genetic modification, for example, is not set out in the Bible even though we are called to be stewards of the earth. We are called to be obedient with every fibre of our being and to offer all that we are in worship. This will mean that we need to make tough calls about a counter-cultural lifestyle that is Jesus-shaped and Christ-centred, and we will do so in faithful and faith-filled wrestlings. These will often be multi-layered and disputed, and in exploring them we engage in the work of discerning God's will. This is precisely the 'faithful improvisation' we talk about in training ministers for today's church as we enable them to imagine new ways of being church and presenting Christ in a rapidly changing world without ever letting go of the eternal truths of the Good News we have received.

So many other examples

It would be so nice (in one way, at least), if this were set out for us in a Haynes-esque[67] manual of Christian discipleship, but this really isn't the Bible we have been given. Just as there is no one way in which I love my wife, even after decades of

---

[67] Haynes Manuals are very practical, hands-on guides to fixing cars and motorbikes, with detailed pictures and instructions

marriage, so we wake each morning to a new day of faithfulness to God in a changing world and evolving life.

So, for example, we give our money freely and generously... but how much, and to what or whom? 10% might be a good guideline, but this is not a law for Christians as it was for Jews. Maybe it is not enough? And how should I actually respond in the moment when I am fairly sure that someone only wants my money in order to buy harmful or illegal substances?

Or how do we decide between two things in the many situations where there is no clearly biblical way forward? If you are a church leader with a traditional view on sexual relations and a new family comes to your church who are married with two children, then I imagine that this will make you glad. If the couple are two men and they are deeply interested in exploring faith, I hope that they would still be welcomed and you would still be glad that they were exploring faith; indeed, that this welcome and gladness would be your strongest response. If they come to faith and start talking to you about how this impacts their marriage, how do you respond? A traditional interpretation of the scriptures would clearly be uncomfortable with the same-sex marriage, but what is the correct course of action that you would commend? Is it better for the children to have two single parent families, with the resulting animosity that all-too-easily ensues as shared life is divided, than to live in one family with two fathers? The easy 'get out' that I have seen employed here is to suggest that such a couple should live together as two single men, but what if this is simply unsustainable in the same manner that Paul grants is true of many heterosexual couples?[68] If a minister insisted on this and the family ended up in painful acrimony when one partner ended up in lusty affair beyond the former marriage, would the minister hold any responsibility for this? Cain tried the tactic of telling God that he was not his brother's keeper, and it didn't

---

[68] See 1 Corinthians 7[9]

ring true even then: the call is to be your brother's brother, not his keeper.

Just to be clear; I am not driving for any particular view here, but I am observing that there are often times where there is not one clear answer that all faithful Christians hold to. Such honesty in the face of really difficult questions is, I find, profoundly necessary if we are to remain humble, human, honest, faithful, real, and growing.

All of this is far from easy, and I realise that I am presenting problems that we can't really solve in any absolute or final sense. That, however, is precisely the point; and it is vital to be honest about it. Christians have always had some understanding of *adiaphora* (things which are of secondary importance on which it is not necessary for us to agree). We accept that different views about baptism are acceptable, for example. I note that it is not only foundational doctrinal issues like baptism upon which we need to be real when it comes to acknowledging the challenge of agreeing what the orthodox view should be in the practical struggle of daily living. If we can hold such tension with baptism, is there not space for other issues to be held carefully? I confess that, when I read the Bible, I struggle to believe that sexuality, for example, is of greater doctrinal significance than baptism... but I also know that this is not how it feels in the church today, and this should tell us something we might be wise to heed.

And while we are discussing sexuality?

When it comes to sexuality or gender, others with far more disciplined and fruitful intellects than mine have wrestled with this and there has yet to be an argument that persuades the majority of Christians. I am very conscious of this as I write, of course, but part of the point of my argument is that any faithful calling requires us to live in this place of standing firm with brothers and sisters in Christ (in the language of Book 1, 'clinging on to them') even when we disagree. I am arguing for a vocation of holding the tension as an act of participation in the missional purposes of God and sacrificial worship.

Personally, I would very much like it if we didn't have to be in this place as it is profoundly uncomfortable and feels unfinished, although this may well be part of the point: here is a way to be in the 'now' as we recognise that the 'not yet' of God's coming Kingdom does actually mean not yet. I suppose I am not sure I can be anywhere else with compassion and integrity. I say this both positively and negatively. Throughout this work, I am arguing my case positively from the Bible and from Christian Tradition, and in so doing building a classic Anglican theological argument based on *'Scripture, Reason, and Tradition*[69]*'*. I also, observe, though, that those who try to construct a persuasive answer from one perspective or another fail to command any degree of unanimity. It might be, and this could be what the supporters of these lines of argument think, that this is simply because some people are wrong. I find myself wondering, however, if it is also because we have a dreadful tendency to grasp part of the answer as if it were the whole answer.

(On which note, please be aware that what you are reading is only a framework within which our wrestling might be able to be held; it is not intended, and neither do I believe it will it prove to be, a magic answer to the questions we face.) Let me illustrate by pointing to a number of others.

Vicky Beeching

We are moved, emotionally and intellectually, by powerful stories like Vicky Beeching's[70]. Whether or not a reader agrees with everything she says or the conclusions she reaches, few

---

[69] This is the classic Anglican tripod upon which our theology rests and dates back, arguably to Richard Hooker (c1554-1600)
[70] Beeching, V; *'Undivided: Coming out, becoming whole, and living free from shame'* (William Collins, London, 2018)

will be left untouched by her story, and I think that most would acknowledge that we are not in a place of settled peace in the church. Moreover, we who seek to wrestle with these questions with any position of leadership in the church rightly feel deep remorse when we hear her eloquent expression of the way that the institution we love and serve has made people feel, whatever our own practice is or has been. We clearly have not got this right, and Vicky deserves our respect for her vulnerability and honesty, whether we agree with her or not. Each of us who follow Christ should feel shame when we read of the torrent of abuse that she has received. It's easy, and vital, to see that we have got some things wrong. Yet, of course, getting some things wrong does not mean that someone else has everything right. When it comes to Vicky's line of argument, which rightly causes us to reflect deeply, we need to recognise that her work does not command unanimity over how we should get things right (unless we are prepared simply to agree with her stance on the scriptures, and not everyone does).

Ed Shaw

Equally, but on the 'other side of the argument' we have works like 'The Plausibility Problem[71] in which Ed Shaw wrestles in an open and honest manner both with his experience and his convictions rooted in the Bible and his walk with Christ. He, too, is deeply admirable and very persuasive both in his lifestyle and his rational engagement with Christian faith and tradition. However, it is equally clear that there are many who do not find his arguments persuasive, just as there are many who disagree with Vicky in her conclusions, and I am not sure that I am content to settle for simple tribal responses to this question. (In other words, it is not enough to hold a view just because some

---

[71] Shaw, E; 'The plausibility problem: The church and same-sex attraction' (IVP, Leicester, 2015)

others hold it, even if they are the people I like or generally agree with.)

I have my own views as you have yours, and there is always a danger that we write off those who disagree with us as some kind of lesser Christian, or possibly as not really being Christian at all. We might even badge this 'good disagreement, but is this really sufficient? I have already noted that we don't do this anymore, at least in theory, when we disagree about worship patterns, or the place of the saints, or the correct timing of baptism, or even the role of the Holy Spirit. Somehow, though, we seem inclined to a kind of doctrinal fundamentalism with regard to sexuality which seems out of kilter. It seems to be of the order of a credal or Christological doctrine (what we believe about the person of Christ or recite in the creeds) rather than comparable to other ethical views we might hold (like the place of warfare, how we bank, or our engagement with greed).

One of the things that Ed is more helpful than I think we might notice (as I am not sure he makes the link explicitly enough) is that the question of sexuality today is deeply tied up with the axiomatic way we hold sexuality as a definitive part of our identity. We talk theology, but live in an unexamined milieu of sexual being. Then we are confused when we are misheard or misunderstood (and this is true for both 'sides' of this discussion in the church even if it looks like affects one more than the other). This is partly why sexuality is such an issue now in a manner it wasn't for previous generations. Moreover, it leaves us with several kinds of questions: How do we expand our thinking beyond our feeling? How do we talk identity? How do we make undefended (and mutually safe) space for engagement with views which differ from ours?

Robert Song

This leads me to think of a scholar (and person) I greatly like and admire, namely Robert Song, and his book *'Covenant and*

Calling[72], which is probably the clearest example of a book that I have read concerning these questions which has offered a new way of thinking in the last few years (although I confess that I, personally, came away informed, intrigued, reflective, but ultimately unconvinced).

At the risk of oversimplification, his argument basically posits that BC and AD sex are different in their nature. By this he means that the purpose of human intimacy pre-Christ has a different and more directly covenantal purpose when compared with the same activities in the new covenant post-Christ.

It is not for me to judge, but the clear logic and theological merit of the argument seems plain to my mind. However, the biblical basis for it seems unpersuasive to many and does not appear to have taken hold. It does not seem to me to be the thinking that shaped Paul's teaching to the Corinthian church in these matters, for example. Again, this is an important voice to hear, and I worry that Robert's work is not widely referenced in our thinking at least as far as I see it, but it does not seem to be a panacea. Perhaps, though, it is the start of a conversation that we have not taken time to explore as fully as we could.

Marcus Green

It is challenging to engage with views that differ from ours without writing either them or the proponent off as some kind of danger. This is one of two key themes that I 'heard' as I read Marcus Green's book, *'The Possibility of Difference*[73], although there are a number of key themes in his writing. Marcus is not arguing that he is necessarily right, although of course he makes his case as anyone would. He tells his story and simply

---

[72] Song, R; *'Covenant and Calling: Towards a Theology of Same-Sex Relationships'* (SCM, London, 2014)
[73] Green, M; *'The Possibility of Difference: A Biblical Affirmation of Inclusivity'* (Kevin Mathew, London, 2018)

asks that he might have a place in the conversation without being written off as an outsider.

One of the many things that I admire and appreciate about his work is that (and how) he directly addresses the biblical text, not least the six texts that specifically mention the question of homosexuality. His point, assuming I have understood it, is that this material on sexuality is primarily about worship not about sexual ethics. Indeed, he would argue that this is the main flow of the argument of the scriptures. I read this with interest, not least because I am more and more convinced (as you will already have picked up) that the main argument of the scriptures is around mission, and I would never want to separate mission and worship.

There is a vital process question here which involves asking who we are looking at as we read the Bible and engage with each other. Marcus is profoundly helpful, at least to me, in reminding us that we only get our perspective right if Christ is front and centre of our interaction with each other. We might not, and I confess I don't, agree with him on his precise interpretation of specific texts, but his main point is really vital; we may not make an idol out of any human thing, even sex, and expect to come out faithful. The text will always be about Christ first and foremost, and this will shape our interaction with our siblings in Christ. I had to smile as Marcus told the story of John Pritchard, a mutual friend, preaching at his farewell service in Christ Church Cathedral as Bishop of Oxford... *'Jesus said, love God, love your neighbour, and while you're at it, love your enemy too. Any questions?'*[74]

Conclusion

So, let's be honest: there is disagreement about whether there is scope within the Bible to interpret sexual ethics with a variety of approaches. I am not trying to convince you of any one

---

[74] Green, M; *'The Possibility of Difference'*, p.118, referencing Bishop John's sermon on 30th October 2014

particular view, but I am trying to expand your confidence in the scriptures and your generosity of approach. Perhaps you can be 'right enough' about something without having to believe that everyone who disagrees with your view is utterly wrong. I hold fast, and sometimes successfully, to the insight that even at my most 'right' I still have much to learn. Certainly there are a variety of views within the church held by those who are deeply orthodox on credal matters of faith and very serious about understanding the Bible. My point is that the Bible is big enough, and real enough, to contain this discomfort and still hold out the Word of Hope.

The fact that there appears to be uncertainty in the scriptures affects all of us differently. For some it is licence to do as they wish, for others the holding to clarity is paramount. For most, perhaps, the path of faithful Christ-like wisdom lies somewhere in between. I suppose my wondering is around how we support each other in this complexity:

How am I the best brother I can be to you when we disagree and everything in me cries out that I am not your keeper[75]? How do I help you to be and to remain faithful when we disagree? How can I walk the path of holiness and wisdom in a manner which inspires rather than condemns, which builds up rather than tears down, which encourages, invites, restores, and delights... and which does all this recognising that I may well be wrong about stuff even when I have got the basics right?

And in all of this I want to notice, and hold onto, two things:

Salvation is bigger than we have yet realised

Firstly, we need to realise how big the grace of God is. It is undoubtedly true that there are a few verses which seem to indicate the limits of salvation, but the weight of the text is clear that the grace of God is never finally constrained by human action. Think of Peter, think of Paul's thorn, think of the

---

[75] For context, this refers back both to Cain and Abel and§ to an observation made by Archbishop Sentamu and recalled in chapter 5 of Book 1

woman caught in adultery, think of the woman at the well. His grace is sufficient. It is so vast that it is clearly possible to be saved even when we live with persistent sin in our lives.

This, by no means, removes the challenging call to holiness. The writer to the Hebrews, who intriguingly remains anonymous, teaches that:

> ... it is impossible to restore again to repentance those who have once been enlightened, and have tasted the heavenly gift, and have shared in the Holy Spirit, and have tasted the goodness of the word of God and the powers of the age to come, and then have fallen away, since on their own they are crucifying again the Son of God and are holding him up to contempt.[76]

Faithfulness to Christ matters absolutely. We must take this seriously. It is essential teaching for any Christian, and any leader, to note. However, each of us lives with unhelpful patterns of behaviour with which we wrestle: if we are honest we will always be on the edge of this teaching because sin persists. We live in a world which demands compromise. By way of some examples: we wear clothes made in conditions that shame us, invest money with banks without asking what the money is used for, and drive vehicles which pollute and destroy the planet. We turn a blind eye to our inner habits and patterns which fall short of God's plan or desire. We know that Christ teaches that to hate is to murder but fail always to constrain our feelings of loathing, or to lust is to commit adultery but voraciously consume media which objectifies a certain style of beauty.

Even Paul wrestled with this:

> For we know that the law is spiritual; but I am of the flesh, sold into slavery under sin. I do not understand my own actions. For I do not do what I want, but I do the very thing I hate. Now if I do what I do not want, I agree that the law is good. But in fact it is no longer I that do it, but sin that dwells within me. For I

---

[76] Hebrews 6.4-6

> *know that nothing good dwells within me, that is, in my flesh. I can will what is right, but I cannot do it. For I do not do the good I want, but the evil I do not want is what I do. Now if I do what I do not want, it is no longer I that do it, but sin that dwells within me.*
>
> *So I find it to be a law that when I want to do what is good, evil lies close at hand. For I delight in the law of God in my inmost self, but I see in my members another law at war with the law of my mind, making me captive to the law of sin that dwells in my members. Wretched man that I am! Who will rescue me from this body of death? Thanks be to God through Jesus Christ our Lord!*
>
> *So then, with my mind I am a slave to the law of God, but with my flesh I am a slave to the law of sin.* [77]

I, for one, am so grateful that the forgiveness of God is bigger than the persistence of my sinfulness. This could be taken for granted as the Romans seemed inclined to do. *'What are we to say? Should we continue to sin in order that grace may abound?'*[78] the Apostle asks, apparently echoing a question from the Roman church. *'By no means! How can we who died to sin go on living with it?'* We continue to wrestle with this, but this verse comes just a few lines before the long quotation above. We live in a messy, muddled, difficult, aspiring, persisting, compromised place. Yet we keep clinging to Christ.

Salvation needs to be kept in focus

And we keep clinging to each other without taking Christ for granted:

> *If you see any brother or sister commit a sin that does not lead to death, you should pray and God will give them life. I refer to those whose sin does not lead to death. There is a sin that leads to death. I am not saying that you should pray about*

---

[77] Romans 7.14-25
[78] from Romans 6.1

> that. All wrongdoing is sin, and there is sin that does not lead to death.[79]

For this is the second vital thing we must keep in mind: there really is only one unforgivable sin. We have already noted this, but we need to keep reminding ourselves. We pray for each other as we fall into sin for *'We know that we are children of God, and that the whole world is under the control of the evil one, [but] we are in him who is true by being in his Son Jesus Christ'*[80] Of course, this doesn't mean we sin with careless abandon as if sin doesn't matter, but still, there is only one unforgiveable sin that is spelled out in the Bible and, contrary to much of what you might hear in and around the church today, the biblical link between blasphemy against the Holy Spirit and genital activity is not a self-evident, direct, or clear one.

Does this mean we carry on regardless? That we are free from the wrestling? That if we sin, we sin? What then are we to say? Should we continue in sin in order that grace may abound?

> By no means! How can we who died to sin go on living in it? Do you not know that all of us who have been baptized into Christ Jesus were baptized into his death? Therefore we have been buried with him by baptism into death, so that, just as Christ was raised from the dead by the glory of the Father, so we too might walk in newness of life.[81]

And herein is the invitation: walk in newness of life. This is not simple, but it is deeply holy, deeply good, and deeply real. Exile does not require either giving in or opting out: it requires faith, imagination, hope, and persistence.

---

[79] 1 John 5.16-17
[80] 1 John 5.18, 20
[81] c.f. Romans 6.1-3

3A - PAUSING FOR BREATH

_____

Pause for a moment and consider. What issues are you wrestling with that have caused you to pick up this book? If the following questions are useful, please use them to reflect:

1) What have I noticed the Spirit of God saying to me in this chapter?
   a) What have I learned?
   b) Where do I want to reflect further?
   c) What ideas will not go away?
2) What challenges does the exilic culture in which I live present to me, practically, today?
3) What is realistic, necessary, and faithful in terms of my own discipleship here and now?
4) What do I need to do in response to what God is saying to me?

4 - LESSONS FROM EXILE

By the rivers of Babylon...
... how shall we sing the Lord's song in a strange land?

Whether this makes us think of Psalm 137 or Boney M's question of 1978 set to its haunting melody, these words echo in the soul of all who know them. Something of the power of the question, calling out over the millennia from its first composition, finds resonance in the exiled heart of the people of God even today.

It is as if we, too, know that we are held far off for now and yet we have tasted and seen that the Lord is God. It is as if we, too, cry: *'My heart is yours, oh my God, and yet I am set in this place which is so alien'*. We hear and echo the cry of the very first singers, Jews held captive in foreign Babylon gathered by the river to offer worship to the God of their forbears whom they have come to know and associate with a land and a temple which is now far off. The exiled people of God cry out: *'how can we sing the Lord's song in this place, in a foreign land with foreign customs and religious practices?'* And yet, of course, even in so doing they show that they are and that they can. They will cease to be who they are created to be if they don't. Their question is so vital that it is captured in the Psalter; in the heart of their people's scriptures and ours. The question is not actually just a question, it is part of our formation as faithful followers. The exiles look to Jerusalem, remind themselves who they are, and rage against their captors.

Identity, belonging, discomfort, pain... all of these are familiar themes as we live in the now of everyday life. All of these were well known to the Israelites worshipping in exile. They are themes which the scriptures seem to deem it OK to struggle around. In saying this, I am simply observing that the clash of faith and daily experience will cause tension and struggle. It is not that God gets some kind of value out of our discomfort, it is that faithful living is hard when others are doing differently. The point is that you can worship faithfully where you are, you can live and express that to which you have been called. Learn from our forebears: don't give up! Their faithfulness would have been their salvation; ours may very well be the salvation of the world. This is a high calling!

We have already explored something of our need to worship and pray in exile, but I do want to note here that this is quite unfamiliar territory for us. In Book 3, we will explore the idea that distance ourselves from powerlessness as a modern church, whether inadvertently or by choice (or both, probably). This is evident in our worship: we do not worship like exiles. More than this, we are greatly impoverished in our unfamiliarity here. In Psalm 137 we see a very raw example of lament with the hatred (and I don't think that this is an over-strong description of the text) of those who have opposed the things of God. We modern Christians are unpractised when it comes to lament and cautious of rage, but both matter in the biblical worship corpus, particularly the former. Worship frames and maintains the theological context for faithfulness in exile: it is the lifeblood, and the lifeline of the estranged people of God, and the manner by which faithfulness may be sustained. It is explored in the scriptures in a far fuller manner than we might at first suspect. However, before we come back to the feast that it will be to explore this, we need to see that there is more wisdom available alongside such a direct exploration. Within this raw worshipping tradition we will look first at how the exiles were able to live faithfully. This is where we turn our attention first.

As in Book 1, where we were considering some of the lessons we can learn from the cross, I will look at this question from two angles. I don't pretend for a moment that this is all that we can learn from exile; rather, I write in the hope that this little chapter will stimulate thoughts bigger than mine, wisdom that embraces, shapes, and encourages, and conversation which continues.

Some key lessons

There are certain key things that leap out of the biblical text when we think about the theme of exile. Remember that we are working with the basic idea that, whilst the exilic theme is constant across the Bible, there are different emphases in this (as with so much) between the first and second covenant. Under the first covenant the people of God sinned, and were taken into exile in order that they might see their sin, repent, and be restored. In Christ, in the new, or second covenant, the faithful live in exile as Christ did in order that the world might see its sin, repent, and be renewed. This is not to say that Christians have nothing around which to repent, but God's chosen methodology of grace is now different.

This first covenant is set out as an axiomatic foundation of the nation of Israel by Moses on the eve of their entering the promised land. He has explained what will happen if the people sin against God, how they will be driven into exile, and then he says:

> *When all these things have happened to you, the blessings and the curses that I have set before you, if you call them to mind among all the nations where the Lord your God has driven you, and return to the Lord your God, and you and your children obey him with all your heart and with all your soul, just as I am commanding you today, then the Lord your God will restore your fortunes and have compassion on you, gathering you again from all the peoples among whom the Lord your God has scattered you. Even if you are exiled to the ends*

> *of the world, from there the Lord your God will gather you, and from there he will bring you back. The Lord your God will bring you into the land that your ancestors possessed, and you will possess it; he will make you more prosperous and numerous than your ancestors.*[82]

We have seen that it is set out with equal clarity for Christians by Peter, and the same would be true in Paul's writings. Think of Paul's argument with the Corinthian church with their infatuation with the super-apostles, and listen again as he writes:

> *For though I am free with respect to all, I have made myself a slave to all, so that I might win more of them. To the Jews I became as a Jew, in order to win Jews. To those under the law I became as one under the law (though I myself am not under the law) so that I might win those under the law. To those outside the law I became as one outside the law (though I am not free from God's law but am under Christ's law) so that I might win those outside the law. To the weak I became weak, so that I might win the weak. I have become all things to all people, so that I might by any means save some. I do it all for the sake of the gospel, so that I may share in its blessings.*[83]

The lived experience of exile, can be very similar in both covenants, and God has not changed: the purpose of exile is life. The lessons we learn from the Hebrew Scriptures are ones on which we must draw if we are to be faithful, fruitful, and joyful in our discipleship today.

1. Exiles are not abandoned

They (we) are in exile for a purpose and still held in the love of the God who has called them and has salvation purposes both for them and through them. We have noted a key difference between the common exilic experience of Christians and the repeated exile of the people of God in the Hebrew Scriptures. In our current situation, we are called to be where we are for

---

[82] Deuteronomy 30.1-5
[83] 1 Corinthians 9.19-23

the sake of the created order; a saved people in a dying world in order that we might be witnesses to the work that God has done in Christ. This contrasts with the repeated warnings about a disobedient people being sent into exile in order that they might see the truth of what they have done and hear afresh the call to return to God and to their land. As is so often the case, the physical reality of the first testament is a picture speaking of the greater spiritual truth. Even here, though, God does not abandon his rebellious people: again and again in the Hebrew Scriptures, we see that God will punish his people but he will not wipe them out. Read Hosea! Look at Isaiah 10 or Isaiah 11, and throughout his writings! *A shoot will come out of the stock of Jesse...* this is great Messianic prophecy, but it follows the repeated pattern of God's call on the faithful remnant who will not be wiped out. God does not give up on his people.

2. Exiles call for repentance

This is evident in the Old Testament, but becomes crystal clear as you read the Hebrew Scriptures in the light of the New Testament. Exiles inhabit a place of repentance for themselves, but also to witness to the freedom of the penitent, and thus restored and renewed life. (Please do refer back to the note on page 60 where we explored what repentance means, as I am very aware it has unhelpfully limited connotations in our modern thinking.)

Jesus comes '*to be a light to lighten the Gentiles and to be the glory of thy people Israel*'[84]. His vocation is to complete that of Israel in setting forth the gracious invitation of God. In Christ this mission is made explicit, but it is present throughout the history of God's self-revelation to, in, and through, his people. This is perhaps most clear in the story of Jonah whose message and proclamation is clear and is to be made at the heart of the Godless power on earth: '*Repent or you will be destroyed!*' Not

---

[84] Luke 2, quoted in this version from the 1662 BCP where it forms part of the Nunc Dimittis.

only is the message explicit, the humorous stark exaggerated tones in which the story is told drum this point home. This is the work and witness of God.

3. Exiles pray for blessing on their host communities

Think of passages such as this one from Jeremiah 29.

> *Thus says the Lord of hosts, the God of Israel, to all the exiles whom I have sent into exile from Jerusalem to Babylon: Build houses and live in them; plant gardens and eat what they produce. Take wives and have sons and daughters; take wives for your sons, and give your daughters in marriage, that they may bear sons and daughters; multiply there, and do not decrease. But seek the welfare of the city where I have sent you into exile, and pray to the Lord on its behalf, for in its welfare you will find your welfare.* [85]

This is not just Jeremiah: the same pattern is evident elsewhere. We tend to concentrate on the Exodus from Egypt, but the history leading up to it is of a people who, even before they are enslaved, have invested themselves for centuries in and for the welfare of Egypt. Daniel served with great honour in the courts of the Persian Kings. Esther thrived as queen of Persia, with Mordecai as a trusted adviser. We will come back to these stories below, but they are common in their theme:

4. Exiles are model citizens

I struggle to think of a single example in the Bible where an exile is called to be anything other than a model citizen in the country to which he or she is sent. There are plenty of examples of battles being won either in open conflict or even by deceit (think of David, Jael, or of Judith in the intertestamental literature), but it is striking that there are no models of civil disobedience or rebellion either in history or teaching. The Maccabee brothers who appear in what we call the inter-testimonial period, about two centuries before Christ, are the

---

[85] Jeremiah 29.4-7

closest I can think of (although they were resistance fighters in their own land so not quite in exile). Whilst they are admired in much of the Judeo-Christian history, they have never been part of the fully agreed canon, and Jesus seems to have worked hard not to allow his followers to follow their example. Even in places where such civil disobedience could have served the interests of the people of God, the way forward which is set out is different. Nehemiah was cupbearer to the Babylonian King, but seeks his favour rather than his downfall. Moses seeks release for God's people but does not incite rebellion. And Jesus teaches the way of peace not of the sword (even to the extent of reattaching ears[86]). The teaching of the New Testament to *'accept the authority of every human institution, whether of the emperor as supreme, or of governors... for the Lord's sake*[87], or to *'be subject to the governing authorities*[88], are very much in line with the entirety of the teaching of scripture.

For Paul, as for Peter, *'there is no authority except from God, and those authorities that exist have been instituted by God. Therefore, whoever resists authority resists what God has appointed, and those who resist will incur judgement.*[89] This is a theologically rational call to model citizenship in order that the mission of God might be promoted.

5. Exiles work hard to stay faithful

It is not true, however, to infer from this last point that exiles merely assimilate, or at least that they are meant to assimilate (some clearly do just fit in, but they are not set up as exemplars). We will see in the following examples that those who are portrayed as role-models for the people of God are those who struggle and yet stay faithful. This is the calling of

---

[86] See Luke 22.47-53
[87] See 1 Peter 2.13-14
[88] See Romans 13.1-2
[89] Also taken from Romans 13.1-2

God, and we see it set out time and again. Listen to the prayer of Solomon when he dedicates the temple:

> *If they sin against you—for there is no one who does not sin— and you are angry with them and give them to an enemy, so that they are carried away captive to the land of the enemy, far off or near; and if they come to their senses in the land to which they have been taken captive, and repent, and plead with you in the land of their captors, saying, 'We have sinned, and have done wrong; we have acted wickedly'; if they repent with all their heart and soul in the land of their enemies, who took them captive, and pray to you towards their land, which you gave to their ancestors, the city that you have chosen, and the house that I have built for your name; then hear in heaven your dwelling-place their prayer and their plea, maintain their cause, and forgive your people who have sinned against you, and all their transgressions that they have committed against you; and grant them compassion in the sight of their captors.[90]*

Exile is a place to work out faithfulness, and whilst this is hard, it is the place we discover grace. I love the pre-echo of the prodigal son *'coming to his senses'[91]* here. Exiles are called to faithfulness, distinctiveness, worship even in a place of cut-off-ness.

This is the teaching we see throughout the New Testament, but which I think we often misinterpret at a fairly fundamental level. Again and again we are adjured to live lives of faithfulness and holiness, for example in Ephesians 5. This is our calling and our command, and at one and the same time we are taught not to judge. We see Jesus in full flight when he speaks against those who lay burdens on others, for example in Matthew 23, but I fear we fail to see that the command to holiness is one which we probably find easier to apply to others than to ourselves. Faithfulness is hard work, but it is our work and we are to encourage each other in it.

---

[90] 1 Kings 8.46-50
[91] c.f Luke 15

6. Exiles dance with powerlessness

In Book 3 of this series, *Dancing with Powerlessness*[92], we will consider the theme of powerlessness as it is a bigger theme than exile. In exile, power is one of the many things that is taken away from you, but Christ invites us to something rather richer than this might imply: he calls us to the radical choice to give away power and be the last not the first, the servant not the master. This is part of the second covenant call to exile for the sake of the lost. It is (sometimes) a choice but we still have much to learn from those who were in exile through no immediate choice of their own. As we learn from powerlessness we will consider these themes further, but for now we note that those in exile learn to compromise, even around deep issues, whilst remaining deeply faithful. They learn to stand together despite their differences, knowing that their very survival may well depend upon their functional unity. Perhaps above all, faithful exiles learn to trust God because they have no other option. This, after all, is the point of exile. I note, in passing, that this is one of the hardest lessons of second covenant exile: do we really trust God for the salvation of those that we love? There are all manner of problems when we do not (as we cannot actually do God's work for him without utterly changing it).

Some biblical examples

So, let's have a look at some worked examples of this exilic faith, how it is lived, and how the scriptures record and perceive it. In no particular order, the following come to mind:

Naaman

I think of Naaman, the leprous commander of the Armies of Aram, who was led to meet the God of Israel by the witness of

---

[92] See little-house-in-joppa.uk/home for details and availability

a Jewish servant who told him that he could be healed at the hands of Elisha.[93] This is one of the most poignant and beautiful stories of conversion in the Hebrew Scriptures, with an almost Christ-like feel to it as we see healing followed by the conversion of life, at least in terms of the worship that Naaman will offer. He takes two mules' worth of earth in order that he can worship the God of Israel at home, reflecting the contemporary belief that gods belonged to places, but makes a specific request: when his master *'enters the temple of Rimmon to bow down and he is leaning on my arm and I have to bow there also—when I bow down in the temple of Rimmon, may the Lord forgive your servant for this.'* And Elisha tells him that he may go in peace.

The first and greatest commandment given to the people of God is that '... *you shall have no other gods before me. You shall not make for yourself an idol, whether in the form of anything that is in heaven above, or that is on the earth beneath, or that is in the water under the earth. You shall not bow down to them or worship them; for I the Lord your God am a jealous God...*'[94], and yet here the prophet permits Naaman to shape his obedience in a manner which transgresses the detail of this command, albeit for a specific reason in a specific manner.

Nehemiah

I think of those who served in high office in foreign nations. I have referred to Nehemiah, the cup-bearer to the King Artaxerxes. We are not given details in the biblical text of the manner in which he lived, but we are naïve in the extreme if we imagine that he lived an isolated Jewish life and yet held such an office. The cupbearer was, second to none in practice, the most trusted servant in the royal household. It was he who drank from the King's cup before the King in order to check that it was not poisoned. He alone would have the chance to add

---

[93] See 2 Kings 5
[94] Exodus 20.3-5a

poison, or permit it to be added, after he had drunk. He alone could pretend to drink knowing that this cup contained death. The King's life was literally in his hands every time the King consumed liquid. Such a man would not be an outsider consorting with unknown aliens. He would have lived, dined, and worshipped in the royal court; and yet he knew who he was and had not forgotten. He knew his God, knew how to pray, and was obedient to his calling. Nothing else about his lifestyle in the court of Artaxerxes is deemed worthy of record by those who compiled his story for our learning.

Esther

Or think of Queen Esther. The same dynamic is true of her, except that in her case we see explicitly that she conceals her Jewish heritage[95] (and thus religion) and that the reason for her obedience being lived out in this way is made explicit by Uncle Mordecai: *'Who knows? Perhaps you have come to royal dignity for such a time as this...'*[96] The frequency with which I hear it quoted would suggest that we love this verse, but perhaps we don't always see it in context. You are here, you have compromised your life and faith in all manner of ways by living in the Royal hareem, you are quite literally sleeping with the enemy, but you are still called to be faithful: now is the time to stand with and for your people and act. Be in no doubt that her concealed Judaism in a highly religious age meant that she partook of all manner of practice and custom which would be abhorrent to the Jews. Her sexual, ethical, eating, and worshipping patterns would all have been shaped by the religious life of the people over whom she had been set as queen. Gone are the strictures of Judaism, but the faithfulness for which she is lauded is still central, and it is faithfulness both to God and to her people. She took her life in her hands, as the

---

[95] Esther 2.20
[96] Esther 4.13

King had taken the lives of her people in his, and acted in order that God's salvation might be brought into being.

Joseph

Or I think of Joseph in Egypt.[97] Again, he is called to be the saviour of the people of his father, Israel. He, too, is living as a senior and trusted official of a foreign nation which was fundamentally shaped by (non-Jewish) religious practice. He would simply have been required to follow these practices, even if only by accompanying others in doing so.

Perhaps we see these events differently because they take place before the law was given, but this, really, is to sidestep the point that God sends the son of Israel into a foreign place and demands that he lives in a manner outwith his covenant in order that his covenant people might be secured.

Daniel

Or I think of Daniel and his companions. Again, we see young men rising to high office in a foreign nation, Babylon in this case. Here is Daniel, which means 'God is my judge', given the name Belteshazzar[98], which means 'Bel protect the King', Bel being a Babylonian God. 'Hananiah' (God is gracious) is renamed 'Shadrach' (Command of Aku, a Sumerian god), 'Mishael' (Who is like God) he called 'Meshach' (who is what Aku is, the moon god), and 'Azariah' (God helps) he called 'Abednego' (Servant of Nego, or Nebo, a god of wisdom). The very names by which these men were called were prayers to gods other than the God of Abraham, Isaac, and Israel. Every time they spoke or acknowledged their adopted identity they consented to blasphemy, and this would only have been the start. They were not likely to have been able to keep Sabbath or to offer sacrifice, their clothing would be made for them and thus wouldn't follow Torahic provision, and they are extremely

---

[97] See Genesis 39ff
[98] Daniel 1.7

unlikely to have been able to celebrate the feasts and festivals of their people. None of this, though, is addressed. The points of 'resistance' and witness are around eating vegetables[99] and praying to the God of Israel[100] and doing so at the right points in time[101], and it is not clear that either of these are lifelong practices. Indeed, given that we see them stepping into their new diet, we can assume that they had to learn to do even these things as they were not normative practice as far as I can see. Yet they are rightly lauded as examples of faith both by their own communities and in the New Testament. The point is not their compromise, it is their acts of faithfulness which stand out, and we do not know why these are the things that they chose to act on.

In the house of Rahab

Finally, I come back to an astonishing and amusing example of this kind of pragmatism and the way that God's faithfulness will be worked out even though we will get it spectacularly wrong as we improvise faithfulness in a far off land. I think of Joshua sending a couple of blokes from Shittim to spy out the promised land in Joshua 1. They are about to conquer this land that God is giving them, but for now it is in enemy hands, and so they enter Jericho in secret, and the very first thing they do is to 'enter the house of a prostitute named Rahab and spent the night there.'[102] Leave aside any moral disapproval you might feel at this, for a moment. It could well be that this is a sensible choice, in one way, as all manner of men would be coming and going from such a house and thus this would be a good place to hide out...

---

[99] Daniel 1
[100] Daniel 3
[101] Daniel 6
[102] Joshua 2.1

... except that these men were Jews, and thus they would have been circumcised.[103] The people of Jericho knew that there was a warring people at their gates and were on the look-out for them. Not to be too indelicate about it, when the spies went into a prostitute's house they would either have abstained from the normal activities of such a place and thus stuck out like sore thumbs. Or they would have indulged in the pleasures offered and their identity would have stuck out... well, let's just say it would have been clear to women rather used to the details of that part of a gentleman's anatomy. Either way they were exposed, they were completely up the creek in terms of concealing their identity. They blew it with their first decision on entering the city, whether through lust, through idiocy, or through happenstance. Their salvation literally rested in the hands of a prostitute and through her God delivered them. Their only trust is in God, and he is faithful. They are not critiqued for this choice, but rather God's faithfulness is shown through it. In fact, there is a rather lovely textual move in the background here: Shittim is only mentioned on four other occasions in the Hebrew Scriptures. On the first occasion the Israelites begin to have 'sexual relations with the women of Moab'[104], and on the penultimate occurrence God promises:

> On that day the mountains shall drip sweet wine, the hills shall flow with milk, and all the stream beds of Judah shall flow with water; a fountain shall come forth from the house of the Lord and water the Wadi Shittim[105].

The place of sexual downfall is the very place of the new promise of forgiveness and provision, and this is highlighted in the final mention in Micah 6, when the people are instructed to recall what happened from Shittim to Gilgal. God's grace is worked out in the far off places and is always faithful, and we

---

[103] This requirement is fundamental to Judaism, both ancient and modern, and is set out, for example in Genesis 17.
[104] Numbers 25.1
[105] Joel 3.18

see it in the life of Jesus' great-great-many-times-great grandmother, Rahab[106].

Conclusion

Exile is a messy and complex place, but it is where we are called to be. It is here that we discover that our faith really is what God says it is and that he really is as faithful as he promises to be. This is not a place of easy answers, self-sufficiency, polished perfection, or sanctimonious judgement. This is the muddy proving ground of salvation and the place where sinners are rescued. It costs everything, and often hurts. It is, though, where Christ is made incarnate, and it is where we are called to be.

Let's turn our minds, then, to the challenge of how we live faithfully here.

---

[106] Mentioned in Matthew 1.5

4A - PAUSING FOR BREATH

_____

Pause for a moment and consider. What issues are you wrestling with that have caused you to pick up this book? If the following questions are useful, please use them to reflect:

1) What have I noticed the Spirit of God saying to me in this chapter?
   a) What have I learned?
   b) Where do I want to reflect further?
   c) What ideas will not go away?
2) What specific calls are placed upon me here and now because I am in exile?
3) How am I going to address these in the next 6 months?
4) What do I need to do in response to what God is saying to me?

5 - EXILE: HOW THEN DO WE LIVE?

So I, often wretched and sorrowful,
bereft of my homeland, far from noble kinsmen,
have had to bind in fetters my inmost thoughts...
All is troublesome in this earthly kingdom...
Here [all] is fleeting.[107]

It would be foolish to suggest that 'exile' is some kind of magic answer to the question of how we live today in the light of the biblical teaching. Exile is gritty, hard, and costly, but it is key. I have argued against the train of thought sometimes evident in the church that says that we simply separate ourselves from those around us who have no faith (see chapter 1 of *Clinging to the Cross*, Book 1 of this series). The creation of mini-bubbles of Christendom is a withdrawal from our mission rather than an engagement with it; it is a denial of the place (and necessity) of exile rather than an embracing of God's call to be cross-carrying witnesses.

I have also argued that we are called to remain holy (see chapter 5 of Book 1) and not simply assimilate. *'Do not be conformed to this world'*[108], instructs the apostle. *'You are the salt of the earth; but if salt has lost its taste, how can its saltiness be restored? It is no longer good for anything, but is thrown out and trampled under foot.'*[109], as Jesus put it. We are in the world, but not of the world[110]: we are a people in missionally-focussed

---

[107] See 'The Wanderer' on page 29
[108] Romans 12.2b
[109] Matthew 5.13
[110] Consider John 17.14-16 for one of the biblical bases for this assertion.

exile. However, we have seen that this is far from straightforward.

In some ways, it might seem that the obvious answer to our question of how we live in the light of this exilic teaching is merely that we live in holiness (and we return to this below). In one way this is absolutely right, except that there is always a problem if this means that our eyes become fixed on ourselves or (worse still) on others; rooting our discipleship in humanity (either lauding it or judging it) is always dangerous. In this chapter, I will argue that the core response to exile is to live in worship in all the rich fullness of that invitation, and do so *both* because it is what the Bible teaches *and* because it makes logical sense.

Biblical responses to exile: two examples

How should the people of God respond well to exile? Let's consider two examples, and in doing so note that they point in the same direction.

Daniel

We have already lived awhile with Daniel, of course, in the reflection that started this book and in the preceding chapter. Daniel's choice to forego the king's food could appear to capture his response to being in exile, although it is interesting that the text does not explore his reasoning for this choice beyond saying that he 'resolved not to defile himself'. This appears merely to be adherence to a kind of holiness code, and in context I think that it is, except that this can be misleading for Christian readers for exactly the reason I outline in the previous chapter; it can make it look as if the focus of Daniel's mind is on Daniel himself. The rest of the book gives a rather different picture.

Twice more in the book we will see exiles make a brave stand. In Daniel 3, Shadrach, Meshach, and Abednego will refuse to bow down and worship the golden image that Nebuchadnezzar has set up (of himself). In consequence they will be thrown into the fiery furnace and their defence is simple:

> O Nebuchadnezzar, we have no need to present a defence to you in this matter. If our God whom we serve is able to deliver us from the furnace of blazing fire and out of your hand, O king, let him deliver us.[111]

In Daniel 6 there is a plot against Daniel and a law is passed forbidding prayer to any other 'god' but Nebuchadnezzar. Daniel continues to pray to the God of Israel, gets caught, and is thrown into the lions' den. King Nebuchadnezzar undergoes a remarkable conversion as a result, of course, which reminds us that we continue to think about mission even though we are considering worship. These reflections are intertwined.

In both instances, Daniel and his friends seek to be holy, but they do so by focussing their devotion on God. Indeed, for a Jewish boy what he ate was (and is) part of their worship just as much as it is part of his holiness. Worship and holiness are inseparable in the text (and in practice), but there is a different focus emphasised depending on where we start: do we look first to God or to ourselves? For Daniel and his chums, faithful exile is made possible by keeping the focus on worship even when cut off from all that usually facilitates that worship. They will face the temple site, they will pray, and they will honour God, even if only in part, by physical acts of devotion.

Ezekiel

Ezekiel is a second great prophet from exile in the Hebrew Scriptures. The shape of the book of Ezekiel is very different from the book of Daniel; Daniel is almost biographical, Ezekiel is shaped around the prophecies that God spoke. Any reading of Ezekiel makes it clear that the behaviour of Israel is a matter of grave concern to God: holiness matters. The nation is slated for its behaviour which is even 'more wicked' and 'more

---

[111] Daniel 3.16b-17

turbulent' than the nations around her.[112] This is the 'reason' given for her being taken into captivity.

However, any reading of the book which stops there fails to notice the point of the book. The book begins, continues, and ends with God's revelation of himself to and through Ezekiel. It is saturated with God's faithfulness and visions of his restoration. Ezekiel 47, for example, speaks of the water of life which will flow out of the temple (and which gets deeper the further it is from that temple, interestingly).

The key accusation that God makes against the people is not that they are wicked, but rather that they are faithless. This is captured succinctly in Chapter 16 which is well worth pausing to read if it is not familiar to you. It speaks of the profound love, portrayed very sexually, interestingly, that God has for Israel, and Israel's utter and complete faithlessness. They are vividly portrayed as a profligate, wanton, immoral prostitute selling their affection to the highest bidder or the latest fancy, and yet without even attaining the value of a call-girl as they didn't get any reward:

> How sick is your heart, says the Lord God, that you did all these things, the deeds of a brazen whore; building your platform at the head of every street, and making your lofty place in every square! Yet you were not like a whore, because you scorned payment.[113]

Holiness matters even when it appears codified, but the core concern is about their relationship with, and thus worship of, God. It is this dynamic, relational, worshipful holiness that I am calling for rather than simple behaviour-led purity. Get the former right and the latter follows: concentrate solely on the latter and God may or may not get a look in.

It is in this broad sense, incidentally, that I am using the term 'worship' in this work, I am not merely referring to what happens when we sing praise to God, wonderful though that is.

---

[112] See Ezekiel 5vv5ff, for example.
[113] Ezekiel 16.30-31

I mean the whole manner in which we seek to glorify God through every part of our lives: our thinking, speaking, being, and doing. I mean the work of lifting his name high, and shaping our being after his will and his way. I mean the whole-life orientation of the self for the greater glory of God and the coming of his kingdom. I mean an expression of holiness that rightly gives him praise and arises from a wholehearted loving devotion to our Lord.

A clear-eyed view of holiness

Holiness matters; however, it is not usually the Bible's starting point. Holiness is not reified in the Bible in the way that it sometimes can be when we focus exclusively on it. Too often we tie holiness to a thing (usually a thing that we feel we can do OK at), and then we become judgmental and critical of those who can't, won't, or don't do it. This is exactly what we see Jesus criticising the scribes and Pharisees for doing[114], and it is not a good thing. In actuality, biblical holiness is more of a reflection of the character of God. It is growing, evolving, and living not merely a code of conduct. If this was true under the first covenant, how much more is it the case for those of us who live in Christ? We live under grace not under law. Only God can change the heart and bring us to a place of holy living.

We might think that worship springs from holy lives, and in some ways it does. We worship as we study the scriptures, discipline ourselves in prayer, feast at the eucharist, and invest in fellowship and offering praise. However, all of these things are God-oriented not us-oriented. In truth it is more that holiness springs from worshipping lives; lives that are oriented to give God his proper place. It is not only in terms of food or clothing that we should say 'strive first for the Kingdom of God'

---

[114] See Matthew 23.23 for one example of this.

(which is code for God's own presence) 'and his righteousness, and all these things will be added to you'.[115]

In this place of worship, you will work harder on holiness than you can begin to imagine, but you will do it in God's strength and looking him in the eye. The alternative is a battle lost before it is begun, striving by your own determination whilst knowing yourself to be a failure. In such a place it is all too easy to end up making yourself feel better by comparing yourself to others' feeble attempts at holiness (and in so doing putting them off faith and selling your own soul in the process).

This all starts with worship (in the fullest sense of the word)!

The primary call to worship

This call to worship, in the rich and wonderful sense of giving God his rightful place in our lives, our living, and our engagement with others, rings throughout scriptures. In many ways it is literally the first and last call we see in the biblical text. This is who we are, and it is who we have always been. It is true for all humanity, created in God's image and invited into relationship with him. It is true for all of us as we will face the final judgement. It seems particularly true, if we are Christ-followers, both created and recreated in him. We are centred in Jesus, rooted and grounded in the Father, enlivened by the Holy Spirit, one with the Trinity. We have been crucified and we live no longer in ourselves, but Christ lives in us[116], our fellowship is not only with each other and with the apostles, it is with the Father, his Son Jesus Christ[117], and his Spirit.[118] This is our identity, sustained, and nurtured as we engage in fellowship with God, as we give ourselves in worship moment

---

[115] Matthew 6.33
[116] See Galatians 2.20
[117] 1 John 1.3
[118] John 14.26

by moment across the entirety of our lives individually and together.

This is where it went wrong for humanity to start with, of course, to return to Romans 1. The root of the human condition, as we have seen, is a refusal to worship, and the heart of the call to salvation is that invitation back into the gloriously liberated space of offering worship. This is where we are united, refreshed, recreated, renewed, restored, and refocussed. It is where we renew our relationship with the One who creates, redeems, and sustains all that we are and all that we are called to be.

Marcus Green makes the same point as he considers Romans 1.[119] I struggle with some of the detail of some of his exegeses but he is absolutely right to centre his reflections on the Christian life around worship. He identifies the fundamental sin of the world to be idolatry, and in this I agree with him. His conclusion[120] is that *it's all about* worship', and surely we must agree: worship is central to this passage, as it is central to the scriptures, as it is to be central to our lives. We are a worshipping people if we are to be Christ's people, and we might feel this ought to be the most natural thing in the world. We would, be wise, though, to heed the warning in Romans and elsewhere that suggests it is harder than we think to remain a worshipping people: we are, at the same time, an instinctively rebellious people and we live in an exilic context which is very far from conducive to worship.

I want, therefore to note two areas of worship that might help resource worship in our exilic context.

---

[119] Green, op. cit., pp39ff
[120] Ibid, page 57

God, the Holy Trinity

It might seem blindingly obvious to say this, but we have been given the gift of worshipping God as Trinity, and if we want to worship faithfully we need to engage with this. There are pressures which chip away at our engagement with every person of the Trinity in a manner which leaves us cautious about engaging with all the fullness of God as we have known him revealed to us. We are cautious in speaking of the Father lest the imagery is too patriarchal or unsettling for those with a negative experience of human fatherhood. We associate talk of 'Jesus' with one part of the church and shy away from apparent over-intimate language when talking about Almighty God in any person. We limit talk of the Holy Spirit even further. I love Alastair McGrath's insight that *'the Holy Spirit is the Cinderella of the Theological ball.'*[121] In reality the revelation of God as Trinity not only reflects the nature of God and engages with our theological preferences, it is an invitation to worship in fullness.

So here is a simple invitation, especially for those times when worship feels a little dry: come and worship the Trinity.

Worship the Father

We worship the Father both in the powerful authority associated with the ancient pater familias[122], and also in his parental loving faithfulness. Both matter and are inseparable, of course, although they often matter at different times in our lives. It is entirely possible that either throws up issues for us, and we need to be very alert to this and deeply kind both to ourselves and to others. It might be that, where you are right now, dear reader, means that you need to park the next

---

[121] I can't remember where I read this, but it captured me then and still rings true with me today. The Holy Spirit is so often overlooked, but belongs at the heart of the celebrations of the Kingdom.

[122] In the ancient world the 'father of the household' (pater familias), who would usually have been father to some of the people there, was the autocratic head of the community gathered in a house with almost limitless power over those who lived there including slaves and servants.

paragraph until you are in a place that you can read it. However, the fact that it throws up issues does not mean that it is not true. Too often we are tempted to respond to human suffering in this area by pulling back from divine truth, and this cannot be helpful if true liberation lies in the freedom of knowing ourselves, as we are, created and loved by God himself.

If someone has been abused by a father this is despicably awful and the very essence of wrong. It will wound beyond description, and self-protection is right and necessary. There are many appropriate and helpful Christian lines of response in such situations, which may well include exploring other images of God, but the fact that humanity abuses and debases fatherhood does not ultimately diminish the perfect fatherhood of God or remove our deep need for his divine parenthood. Indeed, as we engage with God even in the limited ways that are possible for us in the right-now, our relationship with him expands and our understanding of other relationships begins to heal. Redemption and salvation are, in part, establishing of relationship with God and this transforms our engagement with everything; woundedness that we bring is held securely in that relationship and God is very patient, wise, and kind. He is, in other words, just as we would expect a perfect father to be.

Worshipping God the Father is part of our identity, security, discipleship, and liberty. Moreover, we worship with the security of knowing both his creating hand and his sovereignty. We live in the peace of his astonishing love and unfailing protection. We rightly look to him for provision. We entrust those of our brothers and sisters with whom we struggle, for whom we are concerned, or from whom we are parted to the One who is their Father just as he is ours. We worship the Father.

Worship the Son

We also worship the Son, the incarnate One, the Saviour, the intercessor, our example, teacher, and Lord; the author and perfecter of our faith. We worship the God who walks alongside, who understands, who calls, who heals, who waits, who loves. Some years ago, a friend in ministry pointed to many of the modern forms of worship and complained that they were focussed on 'God all-matey' rather than God Almighty. I know what he meant, and the criticism can be fair... but ought always to be balanced. Part of the reason that we need to hold onto worshipping the Trinity is that we live in the space bounded by the awesome holiness of God (which we might associate with the Father) and the intimate muddy-footed presence of God (that we see in the Son). At one and same time we as Christ-followers have the unimaginable privilege of standing with Moses who cannot look on the face of God without dying and with Mary as she kissed the forehead of the incarnate Christ to soothe his night-time colic (or whatever woke him given that in this regard he would have been a perfectly human baby). We must not lose either, even though it is sometimes easier if we pretend we can and only look in one direction.

I remember listening to a powerful evangelical preacher getting carried away in an anti-charismatic diatribe whilst preaching on Deuteronomy 5. Moses reminds the people of God that they had quaked with fear when God had spoken to their fathers at the bottom of Mount Sinai. They asked Moses to listen in their stead for they would surely die if God spoke to them. *'We need to be careful here,'* the preacher said, *'when someone says something like "God said to me..." Ask them if they quaked with fear and begged him never to do it again... for if they didn't then he didn't...'* The statement is etched on my mind. It's a powerful argument for the ungraspable and absolute holiness of God, and a clear reminder that we need to be careful when we speak of the holy. The problem, though, is that the logic of this argument also denies the divinity of Christ. I don't think anyone in the gospels quaked and begged Jesus not to speak to them. And, of course, it fails to relate to the New Testament's teaching on the guidance of the Holy Spirit.

I recount the event because it has served as a painful reminder over the years of the importance of a balanced approach to worship as Christians who base our understanding on our Jewish heritage but who live under the new covenant. It also serves two other purposes which make the story important to me. The first sets an aspiration for me and involves the discipline of searching the whole of the Bible rather than holding to my perception of any particular party line. Whilst I am sure I fall short of this standard, it is shocking how easily adherence to any human epistemological framework leads to profound theological inconsistency. I am quite sure that this preacher held very orthodox views on the person of Christ, and meant no heresy in his absolutist statement, but what he said in this particular pronouncement was sadly and clearly unbiblical, heretical, and anti-Christian. Those of us who teach need to be very careful in our handling of the text[123], especially in those situations where we feel most confident in our own grasp of the material.

The second returns to my theme of how we relate to our fellow Christians with whom we disagree. I still wonder about describing that bit of the sermon as an 'anti-charismatic diatribe' as it sounds condemnatory. I don't want to condemn, but I do want to spot the problem. Ire at another tradition can so fill the mind of a faithful exegete that they are blind to the Christological implications of what they say. Does this mean that I write off the organisation which ran that conference because I was hurt or offended in my reception of 'their ministry'? Far from it![124] The event was basically excellent and I am quite sure that their doctrine of the Christ is orthodox. One of the speakers 'went off on one', and I will challenge that particular comment and the attitude behind it, just as I would challenge their teaching about women, but we still belong together and my task is to love and allow myself to be loved.

[123] We might like to reflect on James 3.1 in this regard.
[124] In fact, the footnote about Deuteronomy 5 on page 38 comes from my memory of that talk.

To do otherwise would blind me to truth about the Lord, Christ, the One who is our peace and who has broken down every barrier.

God Almighty took human nature in all his grace, love, and wisdom, and we are invited to worship. What greater calling could we have?

Worship the Spirit

This leads us to the third element of trinitarian worship; namely that we worship the Holy Spirit. He (or she, if you prefer to employ the grammatical gender of the Hebrew Scriptures) is just as fully God as the Father and the Son. Sometimes, when I speak about this, people object in all manner of ways. There are no prayers in the Bible to the Holy Spirit, I am told. Whilst this might be true, the Spirit has a lot to do with prayer:

> ... the Spirit helps us in our weakness. We do not know what we ought to pray for, but the Spirit himself intercedes for us through wordless groans. And he who searches our hearts knows the mind of the Spirit, because the Spirit intercedes for God's people in accordance with the will of God.[125]

Moreover, prayers to the Holy Spirit occur very early in our history, dating at least as far back as the second century, and I note that we get worked up about this for reasons I do not fully understand. Our God is not three gods: I am trying to imagine a confused heavenly postman wondering what to do with a prayer or a 'bit of worship' addressed to the wrong person of the Trinity. We do have an odd hierarchy of the Trinity which I can imagine amusing each person of the Trinity for different reasons. I know it is a serious matter of church unity, but do any of us really imagine that the heavenly court is divided over the filióque clause?[126] One of the great essential gifts of the charismatic renewal in the last few decades has been the reclamation of the church's worship of the Spirit and an

---

[125] Romans 8.26-27
[126] See note on page 111

apparently consequent relaxation of some of our odder theological scruples in this regard. Let me note, though, that this is not theological innovation as any passing study of church history will reveal.

'Come, Holy Ghost, our souls inspire, and lighten with celestial fire. Thou the anointing Spirit art, who dost thy sevenfold gifts impart.' as Rabanus Maurus wrote in the 9th Century.[127]

'Come down, O Love divine! seek out this soul of mine and visit it with your own ardour glowing; O Comforter, draw near, within my heart appear, and kindle it, your holy flame bestowing...' as Richard Littledale wrote in the 19th Century.

It is not only modern lyricists who can pen lines like *'Holy Spirit, You are welcome here...'*[128]

As we worship the Spirit, in the Spirit, we rightly engage with the very presence of God among us and within us and this takes us beyond ourselves, and beyond the limitations of our own understanding. This is troubling to some, but is a necessary and powerful place of liberty, life, wonder, healing, challenge, hope, joy, and purpose. Here batteries are recharged, life is celebrated, mission is grasped, and strength is sought. Here the head, the heart, the body, and the soul can be let loose in adoration of the Almighty as the worshipper offers love to God with all their heart, soul, mind, and strength. It is no panacea and it is only part of our life-wide and life-long worship, but there is both pragmatism and idealism in worshiping the Spirit. Here is maturity and childlikeness. Here is great theology and the freedom simply to be.

The freedom to worship beyond the constraints of our mental ability is a vital aspect of worshipping the Spirit and in the Spirit. If our first concern is our own grasp of the doctrinal

---

[127] He wrote in Latin, of course, this is a 'modern' English version translated by John Cosin, later bishop of Durham, in 1627 and used at all Church of England ordination services.

[128] This particular line comes from a 2011 song by Katie and Brian Torwalt of Jesus Culture, but is a common theme in modern charismatic worship.

purity of our worship, we will always limit the ineffable God to the horizons of our own understanding. True worship *'in spirit and truth'*[129] will always be a responsive act to the One whose love precedes ours; *'We love because he first loved us.'*[130] If charismatic worship (as we might think of it) gets a bit overwhelming at times, perhaps it is simply an unsurprising consequence of the presence and astonishing work of God. God's presence will sometimes evoke emotional experience. I confess that I have never understood the British critique of emotional worship, despite being very alert to the danger of emotional manipulation. How can our hearts not be moved if we truly encounter the love of God in Christ Jesus our Lord? Emotion must surely be part of worship, whether or not this is comfortable.

This ought not to be surprising either when we look at God or when we look at ourselves. It is inconceivable that we would engage with an eternal God in a manner which didn't include our emotions. It is equally unimaginable that the One who created us and loves us would demand that we lived in imposed emotional repression with all the consequent dangers this brings. We are, I think, often under the illusion that we can control our minds, but fear we cannot control our hearts. This, combined with an unexamined belief that God demands perfection (despite the overwhelming evidence that his desire is for devotion) means that there is little room for error in discipleship. Never mind that this is far from what we see in the New Testament; it is what we expect of ourselves and even more sharply expect from others in the Church. As we worship the Spirit in the Spirit we discover the astonishing, liberating truth that we don't need to get this right to get it good; we just need to look unfailingly to Jesus, and between them the Trinity will sort it out.

---

[129] John 4.24
[130] 1 John 4.19

A note about the place of the Holy Spirit in the creeds
(which is also too big for a footnote):

There is still a major disagreement between the church in the East and the West about the Nicene Creed (or, more properly, the Niceno-Constantinopolitan creed[131]) and the proper place of the Holy Spirit. If you are part of the Western tradition, like me, you will be familiar with saying:

We believe...

... And in the Holy Spirit, the Lord, the giver of life, **who proceeds from the Father and the Son**, who with the Father and the Son is worshipped and glorified...

The Council of Constantinople in 381, which added this paragraph to the Creed agreed in Nicaea in 325, wrote in Greek and their words were:

Καὶ εἰς τὸ Πνεῦμα τὸ Ἅγιον, τὸ Κύριον, τὸ ζωοποιόν, **τὸ ἐκ τοῦ Πατρὸς ἐκπορευόμενον**, τὸ σὺν Πατρὶ καὶ Υἱῷ συμπροσκυνούμενον καὶ συνδοξαζόμενον...

This was translated into Latin by the Roman Church in the late 6th Century, and their translation was:

Et in Spíritum Sanctum, Dóminum et vivificántem: **qui ex Patre Filióque procédit**, qui cum Patre et Fílio simul adorátur et conglorificátur...

There is an issue here; I have highlighted it in bold text. The Greek has the Spirit 'coming' or 'going' 'out of' the Father. The Latin has the Spirit 'proceeding' from the Father *and the Son*, which is the Latin word *'Filióque'*. The Vatican adopted this Latin text as the official version in 1014 and this became a major cause of the East/West schism of 1054, which has still not really been resolved despite some clever

---

[131] For those who like detail, the reason I mention the Niceno-Constantinopolitan bit, is that the Creed agreed in Nicaea in 325 just affirmed belief 'in the Holy Spirit'. Constantinople came back to this 56 years later in response to the needs of the church and adapted it, and the bit we are discussing actually comes from the Constantinopolitan additions.

theological work including a fairly technical statement in search of peace by the Vatican in 1995 which affirms both the Greek and the Latin.

To be fair, this is an issue about the person of the Spirit, and does matter theologically. However, every time I explain it, I find myself imagining one of the endless processions we are so good at in the Church of England, where some get very worked up about their place in the line... maybe it shouldn't, but it just makes me laugh.

The need for lament

This reflection on emotion brings us to the second area of worshipping as those living in exile; namely the invitation to re-engage with a major scriptural style of worshipping which we have almost completely abandoned in the Western church. It is not only the book of Lamentations which does this in the Bible: look at the Psalms! You can argue about exact categorisation, but somewhere between a third and half of the Psalms contain some kind of lament[132].

I am very far from alone in observing this. I would like to quote the great Walter Brueggemann at length as he laments our blindness to the place of lament in worship, but I am not clear about copyright permission so refer you to his work directly.[133] He laments what he calls 'denial' and 'cover up' that seems to him to mark the modern church's practice and be at odds with the biblical practice. For him, faith that cannot 'acknowledge

---

[132] For example, Dennis Bratcher on www.crivoice.org/psalmtypes.html categorises 68 of the Psalms as being or containing lament. His list includes Psalms 3, 4, 5, 6, 7, 9, 10, 12, 13, 14, 17, 22, 25, 26, 27, 28, 31, 32, 35, 36, 38, 39, 40, 41, 42, 43, 44, 51, 52, 53, 54, 55, 56, 57, 58, 59, 60, 61, 64, 69, 70, 71, 74, 77, 79, 80, 83, 85, 86, 88, 89, 90, 94, 102, 109, 120, 123, 126, 129, 130, 137, 139, 140, 141, 142, and 143
[133] Brueggemann W, *The Message of the Psalms: A Theological Commentary* (Fortress Press, Minneapolis, 1985), pp51-52

and embrace negativity' as well as the joy and hope which we know is not really faith in the sovereign God we meet in the Bible. I commend his work to you.

We must learn to lament faithfully as part of our offering of worship. I think I have only really experienced it once, and that only partially as I will describe below, but first let's notice elements of the worship offered in the Bible which we don't often embrace.

Lamentation just says it how it is.

The book of Lamentations begins:

> How lonely sits the city that once was full of people! How like a widow she has become, she that was great among the nations! She that was a princess among the provinces has become a vassal. She weeps bitterly in the night, with tears on her cheeks; among all her lovers she has no one to comfort her; all her friends have dealt treacherously with her, they have become her enemies…
> Judah has gone into exile with suffering… the roads to Zion mourn… all her people groan… there is no one to comfort her. [134]

The Psalmist writes in exactly this way repeatedly, so just to pick one example:

> … evils have encompassed me without number; my iniquities have overtaken me, until I cannot see; they are more than the hairs of my head, and my heart fails me. [135]

There is a brutal honesty to lament which is essential to any healthy relationship. The basic work of any relationship counsellor is to enable people to hear each other. They do not have to be right, but they do have to be heard. This is so important when it comes to worship. How can there be any reality, integrity, or honesty in our relating to the Almighty if we can never speak the truth about how we feel to him or to

---

[134] Lamentations 1.1-2
[135] Psalm 40.12

ourselves. This realism matters; it matters in faith, it matters in worship, it matters to God, and it should matter to us. Lament, though, does more. It will not deny the sovereignty of God in the reality of our situations even when this raises intellectual problems for our faith.

Lamentation is not afraid to ascribe pain to God...

... even if this is not completely right or theologically water-tight. The writer of the Lamentations cries out:

> The Lord has rejected all my warriors in the midst of me; he proclaimed a time against me to crush my young men; the Lord has trodden as in a wine press the virgin daughter Judah.[136]

The Psalmist will ask 'Why, O Lord, do you stand far off? Why do you hide yourself in times of trouble?'[137] or the equivalent again and again. It is God who 'has broken my strength in midcourse; he has shortened my days.'[138] The fact that the Psalmist is secure both in the goodness of God and in his sovereignty seems to mean that there is a fearlessness in lamentation to say that this is God's fault, and he needs to sort it out! Again and again he asks God 'How long... until you sort this out? This is your fault, your problem, and you need to act!'

> How long, O Lord? Will you forget me forever?
> How long will you hide your face from me?
> How long must I bear pain in my soul, and have sorrow in my heart all day long?
> How long shall my enemy be exalted over me?[139]

More than this though...

---

[136] Lamentations 1.15
[137] Psalm 10.1
[138] Psalm 102.23
[139] Psalm 13.1-2

Lamentation offers even the darker emotions

This can be really troubling for the modern reader. Often, in fact, we bracket out these verses when we say these Psalms in the politeness of English (or Anglican, at least) worship. The Psalmist, though, gives full vent to emotions that we do not allow ourselves to have. Listen to what he says of his enemies:

> *O God, break the teeth in their mouths; tear out the fangs of the young lions, O Lord!*
> *Let them vanish like water that runs away; like grass let them be trodden down and wither.*
> *Let them be like the snail that dissolves into slime; like the untimely birth that never sees the sun.*
> *Sooner than your pots can feel the heat of thorns, whether green or ablaze, may he sweep them away!*
> *The righteous will rejoice when they see vengeance done; they will bathe their feet in the blood of the wicked.*
> *People will say, 'Surely there is a reward for the righteous; surely there is a God who judges on earth.*[140]

Do violence to my enemies, Oh God! Some of this might be acceptable to our modern mind as a defensive request. Shattering their teeth kind of asks that they might not be able to attack me, and I don't have many qualms about asking that my enemies vanish like water that runs away or wither in the bright sunlight of God's justice. I get a bit queasier about asking that they dissolve like a snail into slime, satisfying though the image might be if I were really furious with someone, and it really doesn't seem appropriate to ask that someone be like a still-birth. I worry still more, though, at the idea that my friends and I (who are presumably the 'righteous' when I read the Psalm) might bathe our feet in the blood of the wicked. The judgement of God is an uncomfortable place for this Psalm to end.

It does, however, get worse. I have already quoted the beginning of Psalm 137, and we quite like that bit. We don't

---

[140] Psalm 58.6-11

have many modern songs, in or out of the Church's hymn books, that reflect the last three verses of the Psalm, though:

> Remember, O Lord, against the Edomites the day of
> Jerusalem's fall, how they said, 'Tear it down! Tear it down!
> Down to its foundations!'
> O daughter Babylon, you devastator!
> Happy shall they be who pay you back what you have done
> to us!
> Happy shall they be who take your little ones and dash them
> against the rock!*[141]*

Even typing those words leaves me uneasy. I could never condone the murder of infants, and I cannot imagine ever feeling, even in a small part of my being, that it was a desirable thing. Perhaps, though, that is easy for me to say as someone who has never really faced the threat of annihilation; who has never really had a genocidal enemy committed to wiping out all that I love. Maybe that depth of hatred would exist in my soul, too, if you and all that you are existed only to destroy everything I held as precious. Maybe I would loathe everything about you and your culture to the extent that even your new-born children were repulsive in my eyes. I cannot judge, but what I can know is that, if I did have such emotions, the only safe thing to do with them would be to bring them to God, and this is a really vital thing about lamenting.

Lamentation does not need to get it all right

You see, I am not sure I am really the righteous person I am painting myself to be. I have all manner of stuff inside, just as you do, which does not make me proud, or lead me to a confident place of self-proclaimed holiness. The question will always be what I do with this in my worship. Much of it is dealt with in the process of humble confession, at least when I know it to be wrong, but what do you do with the stuff that is all muddled up with your trusting in God? Confession and worship are not an opposed binary pair. You simply don't come to God

---

[141] Psalm 137.7-9

with the bad stuff boxed and ready to give up and the good stuff laid out in praise. You can never separate the grime that we find around us from the pure water of your worship. This cleansing is Christ's work, and we depend completely on it. So come as muddy water *just as you are without one plea but that his blood was shed for you*[142]. If you self-censor before you come to God in worship you will not really be offering yourself. Not that you revel in offering your brokenness in worship, but that you can *only* come broken in worship and your focus is meant to be on God not on you. How do we do this? Lament is one of the rawest and most real ways we come in open trust to the living, loving God, and this is the key.

Lamentation aims its cries at God

This is the vital element both in the lament and in the process it releases and enables in the worshipper. There is a depth of reality to lament which can be uncomfortable to read in the Psalms, but this is not a spectator sport. Lament is an intimate vehicle of communication at the heart of trusting relationship. It provides an avenue through which the broken, hurting, angry, confused, bewildered, or floundering can bring each of these to the God they still serve and love despite the maelstrom within which they find themselves located. Listen to the Psalmist again:

> Deliver me from my enemies, O my God; protect me from those who rise up against me.
> Deliver me from those who work evil; from the bloodthirsty save me.
> Even now they lie in wait for my life; the mighty stir up strife against me.
> For no transgression or sin of mine, O Lord, for no fault of mine, they run and make ready.
> Rouse yourself, come to my help and see!
> You, Lord God of hosts, are God of Israel.

---

[142] To quote Charlotte Elliot's great hymn

> *Awake to punish all the nations; spare none of those who treacherously plot evil.*[143]

This is the cry of one who will cling to the relationship even though it hurts. It is the cry of a confused lover, of a child caught up in emotion that is beyond them. It is essential to any relationship, not least a deep relationship with one who is omnipotent but apparently absent.

Lament is deep faith in action, and is as essential for healthy Christian life as it was for the healthy Jew both on a personal and a shared level.

Lamentation is sometimes corporate and sometimes individual.

The truth is that we need to do this on our own, which might be slightly more comfortable than doing it with others, but we also need to do it together. Psalm 44 is a really good example of corporate lament:

> *We have heard with our ears, O God, our ancestors have told us, what deeds you performed in their days, in the days of old...*
>
> *Yet you have rejected us and abased us, and have not gone out with our armies.*
> *You made us turn back from the foe, and our enemies have gotten spoil.*
> *You have made us like sheep for slaughter, and have scattered us among the nations.*
> *You have sold your people for a trifle, demanding no high price for them.*
> *You have made us the taunt of our neighbours, the derision and scorn of those around us.*
> *You have made us a byword among the nations, a laughingstock among the peoples.*[144]

This is hard to do corporately, but really important. I mention above that I think I have only really experienced this once in a

---

[143] Psalm 59.1-5
[144] Psalm 44.1-9, 14

corporate setting. Much to their credit New Wine, which is a fairly charismatic coalition of churches and Christians around the UK, took the risk of hosting a very different worship stream for a few years in one venue at their summer conference. This explored what worship looked and felt like if it took charismatic theology seriously, but was not bound by 'charismatic culture'. In order to shape this we came back to the scriptures and asked what seemed to shape worship for the people of God through the ages. One day of the week was given over to lament, and the experience of that day was the biggest surprise and joy of the entire project for me.

I have never experienced worship like it, as about a thousand passionate Christians poured out their hearts to God crying out to him for the brokenness and pain of the world and those around them. In the middle of a loud and optimistic conference we witnessed brokenness offered in deeply hopeful faith, and glimpsed what worship truly can be. I knew myself to be on holy ground.

I am not going to pretend that such lament is easy, or comfortable... but it is deeply holy and profoundly good. I don't know if New Wine have continued with this; I do, though, observe that we don't really do much lamenting in any tradition. It seems far easier either to rail against injustice, dance with joy, or proclaim truth...

... the trouble is that we are not at liberty just to do one of these.

Lament wrestles with truth about God and world...

... and refuses to let go of either. To let go of the situation around me would be to lack integrity or compassion, and to let go of God would be inconceivable. There is not the faintest indication in scripture that I am supposed to cloak or dissemble the world when I come into God's presence; on the contrary, this is the world he came to save and he is the saviour, we are not! I can only come as I am, and lament is key to this. Indeed, picking up on our thinking in *Clinging to the Cross* (Book 1 of this series), I would argue that it is the embodiment of cruciform worship. This is exactly what we are called to be and to do, and now we draw near the end of this book, let's notice that (in some ways) it is exactly what I have been seeking to do throughout the extended reflection that lies behind this series. I am not despairing about the situation in which we find ourselves, but I am crying out to the only One who can hold it all; these books form one long lament, really, and I make no apology, because:

Lamentation often, indeed usually, renews commitment, faith, and confidence

I love this. Of all the lament psalms, only 3 are unresolved, namely they end without the glimmer of a sunrise of faith as God's presence appears over the horizon of our pain. Mostly, the psalmist pours out their heart in brutal realism and deep honesty, and through that act of trusting worship comes to a place where they can say *'Yet you have...'*, or *'Yet I will see'*. I think Psalm 40 may well be my favourite of all the Psalms. I love the meandering journey of faith it encompasses, but I particularly love the way it ends:

> As for me, I am poor and needy, but the Lord takes thought for me.
> You are my help and my deliverer; do not delay, O my God.[145]

This captures exactly what I am saying. I cannot see it yet, but I know you, oh Lord, have not abandoned me despite all that lies around. Come quickly and be who you are. Perhaps the most remarkable expression of this is in Psalm 51, where the Psalmist prays *'... let the bones you have crushed rejoice...'*[146] What deeper expression of trust can there be?

I do not understand.

I can't see a way out, around, or even forward.

---

[145] Psalm 40.17
[146] Psalm 51.8

But I will not believe you have, are now, or ever will abandon us.

So I trust.

I choose to love.

I choose to belong to my brothers and sisters.

I choose to proclaim your goodness, that all may come to believe and know that you are life itself, and in you find hope, freedom, forgiveness and grace.

> *I delight to do your will, O my God; your law is within my heart*
> *I have told the glad news of deliverance in the great congregation;*
> *See, I have not restrained my lips, as you know, O Lord.*
> *I have not hidden your saving help within my heart,*
> *I have spoken of your faithfulness and your salvation;*
> *I have not concealed your steadfast love and your faithfulness from the great congregation.*[147]

---

[147] Psalm 40.8-10

5A - PAUSING FOR BREATH

_____

Pause for a moment and consider. What issues are you wrestling with that have caused you to pick up this book? If the following questions are useful, please use them to reflect:

1) What have I noticed the Spirit of God saying to me in this chapter?
   a) What have I learned?
   b) Where do I want to reflect further?
   c) What ideas will not go away?
2) Where and how is God calling me to fresh holiness?
3) How is the Lord inviting me to fresh expressions of worship in my life?
4) What do I need to do in response to what God is saying to me?

A PAUSING AND A SUMMARY

So, where have we got to so far in all of this pondering?

We came into this stage of the journey with Book 1 in our minds and the great calling to be those who carry our cross echoing in our hearts. We may not know how, and we may well not see the future, but we do know that we are called to cling on to Christ and hold tight to those to whom we are sent. At its simplest, this is our calling in Christ and for his world. This is the space between the stones and the firelight that we are called to inhabit.

Here we have explored the biblical theme of exile as a way of helping us live faithfully in this space. The three questions with which we started continue to map the landscape we are exploring, as they always must. How do we remain faithful to Christ? How do we stand together? And how do we seek to be effective in sharing this amazing good news that we have found to be life itself in Jesus?

As we conclude this book and end of this stage of our exploration, I realise that there are at least three reasons that I find this metaphor of exile so helpful in my daily living, as it helps to shape my expectations, hopes, practices, and the orientation of my heart. In Book 3, the next and final stage of this exploration, we will consider the altogether more complex theme of powerlessness, but for now I reflect on why exile continues to matter to me.

Exile shapes my expectations...

Remembering (or realising) that I live in exile shapes the hopes that I have and the demands I unconsciously make of life. It keeps me real, enables my gratitude, and teaches me to ask for help. This shapes many key partnerships in my living as a Christian in the here and now.

... of God...

This might sound odd, but realising I am in exile changes the way I relate to God, at least in so far as it shapes my approach to him. A simplistic understanding of faith might suggest that God's engagement with the world will either be distant (in a kind of deistic, clockwork manner) or controlling (in a deeply imminent, engaged manner). One of the perplexities of following Jesus is that neither model quite works. Exilic space is neither abandonment nor is it fulfilment. In terms of the action of God, either in my life or the work he is doing in the world, I do not need him to fix everything right now, and neither do I need the solutions that do arise to be permanent.

This matters for a variety of reasons; it is hard to live with disappointment directed at God, and even harder when we can see no reason why he would (or would not) have allowed a certain thing to happen. Glimpsing that the space we inhabit right now is 'alien territory' deliberately left for now in order that others might come to know God's grace and goodness of their own free choice, begins to enable us to see that God may well be working far more patiently than we had begun to see. Moreover, when we understand this, we begin to see that it is exactly what was promised to us for now. We often turn to Luke 10 when we preach about mission, and preach about the power with which we are sent. Listen again to the words of that passage (emphasis mine):

> After this the Lord appointed seventy others and sent them on ahead of him in pairs to every town and place where he himself intended to go. He said to them, 'The harvest is plentiful, but **the labourers are few**; therefore ask the Lord of the harvest to send out labourers into his harvest. Go on your way. See, **I am sending you out like lambs into the midst of wolves**. Carry **no purse, no bag, no sandals**; and **greet no one** on the road. Whatever house you enter, first say, 'Peace to this house!' And if anyone is there who shares in peace, your peace will rest on that person; but **if not, it will return to you**. Remain in the same house, eating and drinking whatever they provide, for the labourer deserves to be paid. Do not move about from house to house. Whenever you enter a town and its people welcome you, eat what is set before you; cure the sick who are there, and say to them, 'The kingdom of God has come near to you.' But **whenever you enter a town and they do not welcome you**, go out into its streets and say, 'Even the dust of your town that clings to our feet, we wipe off in protest against you. Yet know this: the kingdom of God has come near.[448]

The whole methodology undergirding these books is to encourage myself (and you, I hope) to read and reread the text and find life in it. We were told it would be like this, for now (and notice that it is like this for the sake of mission). God will never abandon us, but neither will he follow some predetermined formula. We trust him as the good giver rather than demanding particular gifts of him.

... of myself...

Equally, exile gives space to be real as I face challenges and perplexity. Just as I do not expect God to sort everything out in an instant, so I know that I do not need to have everything sorted perfectly in order to follow Christ. Exile is unrehearsed, messy, improvised space. To be in exile is to live in a world

---

[448] Luke 10.1-11

where I do not set the rules and I am not in control. We shall return in the next book to the balance between not being in control and yet still having some degree of agency. But for now I want to notice that realising I am in exile does affect the expectations that I place on myself.

Realistic, exilic expectations make space for us to be kinder to ourselves, and to others. They shape the things that we choose to focus on. I struggle to know how best to express this as it all sounds terribly self-referential and that is not what I mean. We do (or we should) relate to ourselves, though, and many pastoral conversations over the years suggest that we beat ourselves up about things that we have little influence over, and become quite selective about the areas that we focus our development on. One of the great privileges of being 'in ministry' is that the things that are so obvious in others are equally (often more) true in me. One of the gifts of Jesus' insight about the speck and the logs[149] is that when we spot a sawdust in another's eye they can become a mirror enabling us to see the firewood in our own. There will always be things that need addressing in my spiritual life, as there will in yours; realising I am in exile does help me focus on the things I can do something about and offer the rest in prayerful faith.

… of my sisters and brothers…

Exile also shapes what I want, need, and would like to be able to expect of my fellow Christians. At our worst, it can seem as if the church is no different to the rest of society in the way we relate to each other, just as at our best it is amazing to share in Christian love and fellowship. The more challenging and variegated the external situations in which we find ourselves, the more profoundly we need others to stand with and the less important homogeneity is amongst believers. Exile often means that we are standing in different places and facing

---

[149] See Matthew 7.1-5

different challenges to each other, but we belong to each other in Christ.

The most common pastoral conversation I have about sexuality or gender issues, I think, is with Christian parents who are reflecting or questioning because one of their children has told them that they are either gay or trans. I am not sure why I have so many of these conversations, but am privileged to be able to listen. I am not part of that family. I usually do not know the child concerned or even the parent particularly well. Am I there to judge or arbitrate? No.

Am I there to 'solve' the issue they face? No.

Am I there to provide a right answer? No.

Am I there to validate the person talking to me? Not quite that either.

I am often there as some kind of pastoral figure in the Christian community, but primarily I am there as one exile standing with another, wrestling with things that are beyond their experience, holding hands with Jesus and with them, and helping them to pray, reflect, wrestle with the Bible, and love. What we face (here or in any situation we personally find complex, perplexing, or conflicted) is only brought to resolution in the hands of Christ, and the child that they love will only find peace and freedom in Christ.

... and of those around us

It is also true, though, that exile is helpful when it comes to my expectations of others around me who are not Christians. It helps, or at least it helps me, to remember that I am the stranger, not them. My ways are the counter-cultural ones, my expectations are out of line with what most people would think of as normality. I am the one who will be a surprise in the room. People, including me, can only usually see the world clearly (or quickly) from their own perspective, so it helps to remember that I am the one in exile.

It is easy to assume the worst of others if they do not agree with or appear to support us. Recognising that we are the exiles in this context begins to open the possibility of seeing others' responses to us in a different light. People are not interested in being made to feel a minority in their own culture, but they are usually very supportive of those who choose to live (what they would see as) an alternative lifestyle. We are not welcome as judges or rulers, but we are often welcome as sages, poets, healers, and holders of a different space. It is just as big a mistake to assume that the exile is unwelcome as it is to assume that the exile is not an exile.

Exile habilitates compromise

At a late stage of preparing this material, I was due to offer an Advent retreat and used this work to shape the week we had together. One of the bits of feedback that made me think most deeply was that somebody had come into the week thinking that compromise was a dirty word, but had come to see that it was about 'com', meaning with or together, and 'promise' which was a binding commitment to something.

The comment surprised me as I had not really thought that I was talking about compromise, more about faithfulness. However, the more I reflect, the more I think that the feedback is helpful. Life is full of compromises, even concerning the things that we say we will not compromise about, as we have to make things work day by day. We compromise on when we have meals, the way we express ourselves, what we spend our time doing whether at work or at play. Every time we engage with another, pretty much, we compromise as we do not do things exactly as we would have wished to. Indeed, I suspect that we compromise even when we are not with others. I might want to get up at a certain time to pray or go to the gym, but a late night leaves me tired before a busy day. Do I compromise on the sleep I need or on my desire to be up and about? Either way is a compromise.

Compromise is a necessary part of life, the question is not whether we do it, but how we do it well. Realising that we are in exile does not make this question easy, but it does bring it to the forefront of our attention and mean that we can deal with it openly. Exiles do not expect to have everything their own way. Exiles know that daily survival requires engagement with a different culture. Exiles learn not only that they must compromise but that, in doing so, the decisions that they take may well be difficult, temporary, and demanding.

Exile highlights the heart's orientation

Finally, I notice that being in exile shines a spotlight on where my heart is oriented if I will pay attention. At a basic level it often seems that being in a challenging place presents us with a binary choice between God or the world, but I think I am arguing for something rather more subtle than that.

I write this 'chunk' of text as the bishops prepare to meet to discuss Living in Love and Faith. My inbox is overwhelmed with e-mails from every side of the debate about human sexuality. Almost all communications point to the Bible, to the needs of real people, and to our call to be faithful. Quite a few comment on me personally or make specific demands. One, really interestingly, said 'I know that you don't really have a tribe...' and this observation (which may or may not be true, and does say something fascinating about bishopping) has made me think quite deeply about the subtlety of the orientation of the heart in tricky times.

It is all too easy, I fear, for exiles to orient their hearts simply to each other in times of crisis, rather than to that which really unites them. In the challenges we face as Christians living in the modern world, there is a choice about heart-focus, but it is not as binary as it might first appear. I can set my heart simply on the world, with the clear problems that entails. Or, equally easily in response, I can set my heart on the Christian community of which I am part, on my 'tribe', if you like. The danger with this is less immediately obvious, but no less real. My 'tribe' is not God (only God is God). My tribe is not perfect, it does not know all things, it does not save me, and it must never take God's place in my life. When it does, all manner of profound problems ensue. My 'tribe', now I pause to notice, does not unite me with all those whom God calls his children, and this can only grieve his heart.

It is, though, so easy to substitute tribe for saviour. We learn from others, we worship with them, we find Christ together. We confess our sins, stand alongside each other in prayer, and get passionate about mission together. We invest ourselves, giving time, money, gifts, and skills. All of this is, or at least can be, really good. And the positive feedback that we get is from other people. Herein lies the danger, for most people like to be liked, and the tribal appetite for those who will enhance the power of the tribe and offer it their loyalty is immense in pretty much every tribe I have ever seen. It is so easy, even for the best Christian tribes, to lose sight of what they are, and the more passionate they are about faith the more pernicious the potential danger. Just the other day someone said to me (of themselves) in a moment of beautiful and honest vulnerability, *'all of us evangelicals are basically pharisees, and you would be wise to remember that'*.

No tribe can save me; only setting my heart on Christ will ultimately prove to be of lasting worth, and that means that I must be open to making different choices to you, even when you are my closest friend/brother/sister. It is only Christ who can be all in all to me. This should unite us if Christ is Lord to both of us, but we both need to see it and be open about it in order for that to be the case, and even then it will not be easy.

This clarity about heart-orientation can make exile a holy and exciting place, but it is not easy. It may, though, be true to say that exile is not only missional (which has been our main argument in this book), but also part of our own path of devotion, purification, holiness, and grace. Jesus is amazing like that really, but our heart orientation does need to be towards him not towards each other.

Except, if I stop there I have only spotted one of the dangers of the orientation of the heart in exile, for I could be arguing that the only way to do this is alone. It could seem that I am saying that we have a choice between faithlessness (either by siding with the world or by belonging more to our tribe than we do to Christ) or an isolated personal devotion to Christ which is impervious to those around. If I cannot set my heart on the world, and I cannot set my heart on you (as my brother or sister in Christ) and the 'tribe' that we are part of, does that mean that I must stand alone looking only to Christ? If this pendulum swings completely to individualism and isolated holiness we have simply replaced one problem with another. We were never intended to walk the Christian life alone. The Bible is very clear that we need each other.

This insight can help us to reflect on the health of the fellowship in which we walk, and into which we invite others. It is said of your 'rut' that you should choose it with care as you will be stuck in it for years, and I think the same may be true, unless we are very careful, of the fellowship we choose to keep in the church. Maybe my correspondent (above) had spotted a helpful thing about being bishop; we span multiple Christian communities and are invited to care for all of them, but the basic insight matters for us all.

There are certain things that I have noticed I begin to ask when I am with strongly flavoured groups. When they pray, is there humility present? When they read the Bible, is it serving them or are they sitting under the actual text? Are they kind? Are they patient? Are they interested? I find myself needing to ask whose purpose is served by this fellowship or that? I am rather more interested in how a group respond to outsiders than their behaviour towards fellow 'tribe members'. I begin to notice whether I am more or less focussed on Christ when I have spent time with people from particular groups. I am not good when it feels like the system simply wants to control or use me for its own purpose. Perhaps above all nowadays, I find myself noticing whether I know more about what a group stands for than I do what it stands against. There are many battles that it is worth fighting, but internal squabbles are neither edifying nor useful.

Will you help me, and let me help you, orient your heart to Christ? Here we will find hope. Here we will find strength. Here, as we seek first His Kingdom, will all things be added to us.[150]

Two final thoughts: I am intrigued (and slightly amused) that it has taken me this long to note these observations about tribes. The power of a tribe is greater than we realise and I am not sure that I was in a place to offer such reflections earlier, and neither might you have been in a place to hear it. This is potentially unsettling stuff, but it is important. Secondly, please note that I offer this insight not to take people out of groups, or groups out of the church, but rather to help groups become more reflective. We need each other and we are social people, it is simply that we are Christ's social people above and beyond all things. This matters at all times, but exile quickly becomes wilderness when we forget our need of each other.

We belong, in all things and for all time, to Christ. He is our hope, our inheritance, our saviour, our guide, our example, and our Lord. We follow him into exile, and there we discover the freedom and unity of living as aliens and strangers for the sake of the salvation of this world. This is far from straightforward and there are real questions about how we live faithfully. What is it that shapes our imagination, our prayer, our worship, and our practice?

---

[150] See Matthew 6.33

In Book 1 we looked back to glimpse again our fundamentally cruciform nature as a people held together by the cross of Christ. Here, in this book, we have wrestled with our call into exile. In the third and final book of this series we shall look at powerlessness, the outline of our approach and engagement with each other and the world. We have struggled, in the Western Church, to remember this for 1700 years, which possibly makes this the hardest of our three fundamental metaphors. It is, though, vital to faithfulness in the modern world. There, as here, we note that it is only in standing together that we are able to face all that lies ahead of us.

All for Jesus! all for Jesus!
This our song shall ever be:
you our only hope, our Saviour,
yours the love that sets us free!

All for Jesus: you will give us
strength to serve you hour by hour;
none can move us from your presence
while we trust your grace and power.

(WJ Sparrow-Simpson, 1887)

EPILOGUE

You might like to listen to this before reading on
(it was designed to be heard more than read), but it's up to
you.

It was a great fire in an expensive brazier in that magnificent courtyard... and a terrible place to be. One of those times when you are not sure which is hotter, the flames or the tempers; which more incendiary, the sparks settling on dusty clothing, or the sparks settling in wounded hearts; which flickered more dramatically, the firelight or our will to live. On that evening without hope in the darkness and the shifting light of flames that had lost the ability to dance.

We had gathered. Well, they had gathered and I had delivered firewood as demanded and was hanging around for food. Accusations were being thrown around in that way that men so often do it. Banter. Jokes. A word out of place. You were one of his mates weren't you? I recognise your accent. I saw you with him.

And the denials flew quicker than the mind could move, than the words could contain, than the spittle flying from enraged lips, than the fists clenched and would have been thrown were it not for those soldiers. No amount of food is worth this.

And so we cowered, and pretended we could not hear the punishments being meted out elsewhere or the legal arguments at the front, or the violent recriminations right in front of us.

Until the cock crowed and the eyes met, and silence struck harder than the blows falling on already bleeding backs.

I will never forget the look in his eyes…

… the eyes that I can hardly see tonight in the pain of that broken face on a cowed and dejected body.

Here, by coincidence… as I am in this different space, this beach space, this quiet place with no expensive brazier or crowing crowds… here, gathering driftwood and doing a favour for that man who reminded me of the silent convicted bloke on that other night. He needed a hand with a lump too big for him to carry alone and he was so kind, I couldn't help smiling when he greeted his mates in their boat.

And now those eyes… so angry on that night, now not able to look up… at the fire… at me… at him. He did not just look like him you know. He moved like him, sounded like him. He even had scars like him now I think of it. Weird that.

He was back there too… the man with the eyes… in front of this new fire, this simpler but heavenly smelling food… now on the beach not in the courtyard. Now in what should have been peace, not in conflict.

Simon… that must have been his name… son of John, do you love me?

He was very fixated on that question, you know. Over and over he asked it, but not like a bully, or a drunk, or a loon. With patient deliberation just like…

... well actually just like that rooster crowed as if to mock the insistent denial: I do not know this man. I do not, I don't... I remember it so clearly now. But these questions were not mocking. So very not mocking.

Asked by the broken one who was no longer broken and was unimaginably ridiculously beautifully here. Holding the breaking broken one who could not look himself in the eye let alone anyone else. Speaking into the dwindling devastating darkness with impossible hope... and teaching the flames to dance one flicker at a time.

Do - you - love - me.

I do, I do, I do... and with each carefully crafted and affirmed affirmation held between the two who were more one than ever before... in this place something came back to life. Alive but not simply restored. Remade more like. Made new. Better than new somehow. Repurposed. Recommissioned. Retrusted. Revitalised. Recrafted. Reloved. Revealed. Renewed.

Like a community was birthed... or a movement... or a way... or a people... or a kingdom.

It wasn't much of a fire, or much of a beach to be frank... but as the campfire's embers glowed in that improvised hearth and seemed to foretell a greater coming feast in a far off place that echoed in their words... it was the most amazing place to be.

BIBLE REFERENCES

James 3.1   107

THE STONES AND FIRELIGHT SERIES

Little House in Joppa are pleased to offer the 'Stones and Firelight' series, of which this book is the second. All three books are (or will be) available in printed and electronic form.

There is (or will be) accompanying study group material with additional podcast material for each book: please use the link below to find out more.

Book 1: *Clinging to the Cross* (LHIJ, 2023)

      ISBN (Paperback):   978-1-7392688-0-0

      ISBN (E-book)   978-1-7392688-3-1

Book 2: *Called into Exile* (LHIJ, 2023)

      ISBN (Paperback):   978-1-7392688-1-7

      ISBN (E-book)   978-1-7392688-4-8

Book 3: *Dancing with Powerlessness* (Due late 2023)

      ISBN (Paperback):   978-1-7392688-2-4

      ISBN (E-book)   978-1-7392688-5-5

Stones and Firelight resources

For study material and other resources, from Little House in Joppa please visit:

little-house-in-joppa.uk/S&FResources

(This the page will be updated as further material becomes available)

Printed in Great Britain
by Amazon

47326200R00088